Edward Arber

The Pope anthology

1701-1744 AD

Edward Arber

The Pope anthology
1701-1744 AD

ISBN/EAN: 9783743306820

Manufactured in Europe, USA, Canada, Australia, Japa

Cover: Foto ©Thomas Meinert / pixelio.de

Manufactured and distributed by brebook publishing software (www.brebook.com)

Edward Arber

The Pope anthology

THE POPE ANTHOLOGY.

1701–1744 A.D.

EDITED BY

Professor EDWARD ARBER, F.S.A.,

FELLOW OF KING'S COLLEGE, LONDON, ETC.

> 'A thing of beauty is a joy for ever;
> Its loveliness increases.'
> KEATS.

LONDON:
HENRY FROWDE,
OXFORD UNIVERSITY PRESS WAREHOUSE, AMEN CORNER, E.C.
NEW YORK: 91 & 93 FIFTH AVENUE.
1899.

Contents.

	PAGE
HOWARD, Earl of SUFFOLK (1671-1731); EDWARD	200, 201
LEVERIDGE (1670-1758); RICHARD	262-264
LYTTELTON, Lord LYTTELTON (1709-1773); GEORGE	244-250
[? MALLET (1705-1765); DAVID	278, 279]
MILLER (1706-1744); Rev. JAMES	265
MONK (c. 1716); Hon. MARY	137
MONTAGU (1689-1762); Lady MARY (PIERREPONT, afterwards) WORTLEY	143-146, 152-155
MORDAUNT, Earl of PETERBOROUGH (1658-1735); CHARLES	225
MOTTEUX (1660-1718); PIERRE ANTOINE	66, 67
PAGET, Lord PAGET (1689-1742); THOMAS CATESBY	292, 293
PARNELL, D.D., Archdeacon of Clogher (1679-1718); THOMAS	114-120
PHILIPS (1675-1749); AMBROSE	104-108
PHILIPS (1676-1709); JOHN	93
POPE (1688-1744); ALEXANDER	1-36, 46, 47, 109, 150, 151
POPPLE (1701-1764); WILLIAM	251
PRIOR (1664-1721); MATTHEW	68-92
R., S. (c. 1724)	194, 195
RAMSAY (1686-1758); ALLAN	181-185
ROOME (? -1729); EDWARD	218-220
ROWE, Poet Laureate (1674-1718); NICHOLAS	124-127
SAVAGE (? -1743); RICHARD	206, 207
SHEFFIELD, Duke of BUCKINGHAM (1648-1721); JOHN	131-135
SOMERVILLE (1675-1742); WILLIAM	214-217
STEELE (1672-1729); Captain Sir RICHARD	62, 63
SWIFT, Dean of St. Patrick's Cathedral, Dublin (1667-1745); JONATHAN	210-213
THOMSON (1700-1748); JAMES	278-284
THURSTON (c. 1729); JOSEPH	226, 227
TICKELL (1686-1740); THOMAS	172-174
WALSH (1663-1708); WILLIAM	52-54
WARD (1667-1731); EDWARD	175-177
WELSTED (1689-1747); LEONARD	138, 139
WESLEY the Elder (1692-1739); Rev. SAMUEL	199
WEST, the friend of THOMAS GRAY (? -1642); RICHARD	285-287
WILLIAMS, Knight of the Bath (1709-1759); Sir CHARLES HANBURY	288-291
YONGE, Bart. (? -1775); Rt. Hon. Sir WILLIAM	236, 237
FIRST LINES AND NOTES	301
GLOSSARY AND INDEX	307

THE POPE ANTHOLOGY.

1701–1744 A.D.

ON A CERTAIN LADY AT COURT.

[HENRIETTA HOWARD, COUNTESS OF SUFFOLK.]

I KNOW the thing that's most uncommon!
   (ENVY, be silent; and attend!)
I know a reasonable woman;
   Handsome and witty, yet a friend!

Not warped by passion, awed by rumour;
   Not grave through pride, or gay through folly;
An equal mixture of good humour
   And sensible soft melancholy.

'Has she no faults then,' ENVY says, 'Sir?'
   Yes, she has one, I must aver!
When all the World conspires to praise her;
   The woman's deaf, and does not hear!

Alexander Pope.

ODE ON SOLITUDE.

[This imitation of HORACE's Ode, *Beatus integer*, &c., was written in 1700, when young ALEXANDER POPE was not twelve years old. The present is his revised text of 1736.]

HAPPY the man! whose wish and care
   A few paternal acres bound;
Content to breathe his native air
      In his own ground:

Whose herds, with milk; whose fields, with bread;
   Whose flocks supply him with attire:
Whose trees, in Summer yield him shade;
      In Winter, fire.

Blest! who can unconcern'dly find
   Hours, days, and years slide soft away
In health of body, peace of mind,
      Quiet by day,

Sound sleep by night; study and ease
   Together mixt; sweet recreation;
And innocence, which most does please,
      With meditation.

Thus, let me live, unseen! unknown!
   Thus, unlamented, let me die!
Steal from the world; and not a stone
      Tell where I lie!

Alexander Pope.

THESE, equal syllables alone require;
Though oft, the ear the open vowels tire!
While expletives, their feeble aid do join;
And ten low words oft creep in one dull line;
While they ring round the same unvaried chimes,
With sure returns of still expected rhymes.
Where'er you find *the cooling western breeze*,
In the next line, it *whispers through the trees.*
If *crystal streams with pleasing murmurs creep*,
The Reader's threatened, not in vain, with *sleep.*
Then, at the last, and only couplet fraught
With some unmeaning thing they call a thought,
A needless Alexandrine ends the Song,
That, like a wounded snake, draws its slow length along.
    Leave such to tune their own dull rhymes; and know
What's roundly smooth, or languishingly slow!
And praise the easy vigour of a line,
Where DENHAM's strength and WALLER's sweetness join!
    [True ease in writing comes from art, not chance;
As those move easiest who have learned to dance.]
'Tis not enough, no harshness gives offence;
The Sound must seem an echo to the Sense!
    Soft is the strain when ZEPHYR gently blows;
And the smooth stream, in smoother Numbers flows:
But when loud surges lash the sounding shore,
The hoarse rough Verse should, like the torrent, roar!
    When AJAX strives, some rock's vast weight to throw,
The line too labours, and the words move slow:
Not so, when swift CAMILLA scours the plain;
Flies o'er th' unbending corn, and skims along the Main.

Alexander Pope.

POPE wrote but few short Poems that are suitable for this Series. In order, therefore, to do him justice, one of his longer pieces is here given; and *The Rape of the Lock* for preference, because, as regards its form, it is one of the masterpieces of English Mock Heroic Verse; while its subject matter gives us a charming picture of the Age of Queen ANNE.

This Poem is in English, what BOILEAU's *Lutrin* is in French. It is based upon an incident in real life; and the characters in it are

BELINDA, Mrs. ARABELLA FERMOR.
The Baron, Lord PETRE.
THALESTRIS, Mrs. MORLEY.
Sir *PLUME*, her brother, Sir George BROWN.
CLARISSA.

While there is much fun and burlesque pomposity in the Poem, it contains not a few exquisitely musical lines; and, in other respects, carries out the principles of writing verse that POPE has laid down on the preceding page. It is also a sufficiently acid banter of the Fair Sex; so that Lady WINCHILSEA, at page 111, advises POPE to 'soothe the Ladies!'

THE RAPE OF THE LOCK.

AN HEROI-COMICAL POEM
IN FIVE CANTOS.

A tonso est hoc nomen adepta capillo.—OVID.

Nolueram, BELINDA [POLYTIMUS] *tuos violare capillos:
Sed juvat hoc precibus me tribuisse tuis.*—MARTIAL.

CANTO I.

WHAT dire offence, from am'rous causes springs,
What mighty quarrels rise from trivial things;
I sing! This Verse to CARYL, Muse! is due!
This, ev'n BELINDA may vouchsafe to view!
Slight is the subject; but not so the praise,
If she inspire, and he approve, my Lays!

Say, what strange motive, Goddess! could compel
A well-bred Lord t' assault a gentle Belle?
O, say, what stranger cause, yet unexplored,
Could make a gentle Belle reject a Lord?
And dwells such rage in softest bosoms then?
And lodge such daring souls in little men?

Sol, through white curtains, did his beams display;
And oped those eyes, which brighter shine than they.
Now Shock had given himself the rousing shake;
And Nymphs prepared their chocolate to take.
Thrice the wrought slipper knocked against the ground;
And striking watches the tenth hour resound.
BELINDA still her downy pillow prest:
Her guardian Sylph prolonged the balmy rest.
'Twas he had summoned to her silent bed
The Morning Dream that hovered o'er her head.
A Youth, more glitt'ring than a Birth-night Beau,
(That ev'n in slumber caused her cheek to glow!)
Seemed to her ear, his winning lips to lay;
And thus, in whispers said, or seemed to say.
'Fairest of mortals! thou distinguished care
Of thousand bright inhabitants of air!
If e'er one vision touched thy infant thought
Of all the Nurse, and all the Priest, have taught
Of airy Elves by moonlight shadows seen,
The silver token, and the circled Green;
Or Virgins visited by Angel Powers,
With golden crowns and wreaths of heavenly flowers;

Alexander Pope.

Hear, and believe! Thy own importance know;
Nor bound thy narrow views to things below!
Some secret truths, from learned Pride concealed,
To maids alone and children are revealed!
What though no credit doubting Wits may give;
The Fair and Innocent shall still believe!

'Know then, unnumbered Spirits round thee fly!
The light Militia of the lower sky!
These, though unseen, are ever on the wing,
Hang o'er the Box, and hover round the Ring.

'Think what an equipage thou hast in air;
And view with scorn two Pages and a Chair!
As now your own, our Beings were of old;
And once inclosed in Woman's beauteous mould:
Thence, by a soft transition, we repair
From earthly vehicles to these of air.

'Think not, when Woman's transient breath is fled,
That all her vanities at once are dead!
Succeeding vanities she still regards;
And, though she plays no more, o'erlooks the cards!
Her joy in gilded Chariots, when alive,
And love of Ombre, after death survive!

'For when the Fair in all their pride expire,
To their first Elements the souls retire!
The Sprights of fiery termagants in flame
Mount up, and take a Salamander's name.
Soft yielding minds to water glide away;
And sip with Nymphs their Elemental tea.
The graver Prude sinks downward to a Gnome,
In search of mischief still on earth to roam.

Alexander Pope.

The light Coquettes in Sylphs aloft repair,
And sport and flutter in the fields of air.
 'Know farther yet, Whoever fair and chaste
Rejects Mankind, is by some Sylph embraced;
For Spirits, freed from mortal laws, with ease
Assume what sexes, and what shapes, they please.
 'What guards the purity of melting Maids
In Courtly Balls, and midnight Masquerades,
Safe from the treach'rous friend, and daring Spark,
The glance by day, the whisper in the dark,
When kind occasion prompts their warm desires,
When Music softens, and when Dancing fires?
'Tis but their Sylph, the wise celestials know;
Though Honour is the word with men below.
 'Some Nymphs there are, too conscious of their face,
For life predestined to the Gnomes' embrace:
Who swell their prospects, and exalt their pride;
When offers are disdained, and love denied.
Then, gay ideas crowd the vacant brain,
While Peers and Dukes, and all their sweeping Train,
And Garters, Stars, and Coronets appear,
And, in soft sounds, "Your Grace!" salutes their ear.
'Tis these, that early taint the female soul,
Instruct the eyes of young Coquettes to roll,
Teach infants' cheeks, a bidden blush to know;
And little hearts to flutter at a Beau!
 'Oft when the World imagine women stray,
The Sylphs through mystic mazes guide their way!
Through all the giddy circle they pursue,
And old impertinence expel by new!

What tender Maid but must a victim fall
To one man's treat, but for another's Ball?
When FLORIO speaks, what Virgin could withstand,
If gentle DAMON did not squeeze her hand?
With varying vanities, from ev'ry part,
They shift the moving Toyshop of their heart;
Where wigs with wigs, with sword-knots, sword-knots strive;
Beaus banish Beaus; and coaches, coaches drive.
This, erring mortals Levity may call.
O, blind to Truth! The Sylphs contrive it all!
  'Of these am I, who thy protection claim;
A watchful Sprite, and ARIEL is my name.
Late, as I ranged the crystal wilds of air,
In the clear mirror of thy ruling star
I saw, alas! some dread event impend,
Ere to the Main this morning's sun descend!
But Heaven reveals not What, or How, or Where.
  'Warned by thy Sylph, O, pious Maid! beware!
This to disclose is all thy Guardian can!
Beware of all! but most beware of Man!'

  He said: when Shock, who thought she slept too long,
Leapt up, and waked his Mistress with his tongue.
  'Twas then, BELINDA! if report say true,
Thy eyes first opened on a *billet-doux*.
Wounds, charms, and *ardours* were no sooner read;
But all the vision vanished from thy head!

Alexander Pope.

   And now, unveiled, the Toilet stands displayed;
Each silver vase in mystic order laid.
First, robed in white, the Nymph intent adores,
With head uncovered, the Cosmetic Powers.
A heavenly image in the Glass appears;
To that she bends, to that her eyes she rears.
   Th' inferior Priestess, at her altar's side,
Trembling begins the sacred rites of Pride.
Unnumbered treasures ope at once; and here
The various off'rings of the world appear.
From each she nicely culls, with curious toil,
And decks the Goddess with the glitt'ring spoil!
This casket, India's glowing gems unlocks;
And all Arabia breathes from yonder box!
The tortoise here and elephant unite,
Transformed to combs, the speckled and the white
Here files of pins extend their shining rows,
Puffs, powders, Patches, *Bibles, billets-doux.*
   Now, awful Beauty puts on all its Arms;
The Fair, each moment, rises in her charms!
Repairs her smiles, awakens ev'ry grace,
And calls forth all the wonders of her face!
Sees, by degrees, a purer blush arise;
And keener lightnings quicken in her eyes!
   The busy Sylphs surround their darling care.
These set the head, and those divide the hair;
Some fold the sleeve, while others plait the gown:
And BETTY's praised for labours not her own!

THE RAPE OF THE LOCK.

CANTO II.

Not with more glories in th' ethereal plain,
The sun first rises o'er the purpled Main,
Than, issuing forth, the Rival of his beams
Launched on the bosom of the silver Thames.
Fair Nymphs and well-dressed Youths around her shone;
But ev'ry eye was fixed on her alone.
On her white breast, a sparkling cross she wore;
Which Jews might kiss, and Infidels adore!
Her lively looks a sprightly mind disclose;
Quick as her eyes, and as unfixed as those.
Favours to none, to all she smiles extends;
Oft she rejects, but never once offends.
Bright as the sun, her eyes the gazers strike;
And, like the sun, they shine on all alike.

Yet graceful ease, and sweetness void of pride,
Might hide her faults, if Belles had faults to hide!
If to her share some female errors fall;
Look on her face, and you'll forget them all!

This Nymph, to the destruction of Mankind,
Nourished two Locks; which graceful hung behind
In equal curls, and well conspired to deck
With shining ringlets her smooth iv'ry neck.
LOVE in these labyrinths his slaves detains;
And mighty hearts are held in slender chains.
With hairy springes we the birds betray.
Slight lines of hair surprise the finny prey.
Fair tresses Man's imperial race insnare;
And Beauty draws us with a single hair.

Th' adventurous Baron, the bright locks admired.
He saw, he wished, and to the prize aspired!
Resolved to win; he meditates the way,
By force to ravish, or by fraud betray.
For when success a Lover's toil attends,
Few ask, 'If fraud, or force, attained his ends?'

For this, ere PHŒBUS rose, he had implored
Propitious Heaven; and ev'ry Power adored!
But chiefly, LOVE! To LOVE, an altar built
Of twelve vast French Romances, neatly gilt.

Alexander Pope.

There, lay the sword-knot SYLVIA's hands had sown;
With FLAVIA's busk, that oft had rapped his own.
A fan, a garter, half a pair of gloves,
And all the trophies of his former Loves.
    With tender *billets-doux* he lights the pyre;
And breathes three am'rous sighs to raise the fire.
Then prostrate falls; and begs with ardent eyes
Soon to obtain, and long possess, the prize.
    The Powers gave ear, and granted half his prayer;
The rest, the winds dispersed in empty air!

    But now secure the painted vessel glides,
The sunbeams trembling on the floating tides;
While melting music steals upon the sky,
And softened sounds along the waters die.
Smooth flow the waves, the zephyrs gently play;
BELINDA smiled, and all the World was gay!

    All but the Sylph! With careful thoughts opprest,
Th' impending woe sat heavy on his breast.
    He summons straight his denizens of Air.
The lucid squadrons round the Sails repair.
Soft o'er the Shrouds aerial whispers breathe,
That seemed but zephyrs to the Train beneath.
Some to the sun their insect-wings unfold,
Waft on the breeze, or sink in clouds of gold.
Transparent Forms, too fine for mortal sight,
Their fluid bodies half dissolved in light.

Loose to the wind their airy garments flew,
Thin glitt'ring textures of the filmy dew
Dipped in the richest tincture of the skies,
Where light disports in ever-mingling dyes;
While ev'ry beam new transient colours flings,
Colours that change, whene'er they wave their wings.

Amid the circle, on the gilded Mast,
Superior by the head, was ARIEL placed;
His purple pinions opening to the sun.
He raised his azure wand, and thus begun.
　'Ye Sylphs and Sylphids! to your Chief give ear!
Fays, Fairies, Genii, Elves, and Dæmons, hear!
Ye know the spheres and various tasks assigned,
By laws eternal, to th' aerial kind!
　'Some in the fields of purest ether play;
And bask and whiten in the blaze of day.
Some guide the course of wand'ring orbs on high;
Or roll the Planets through the boundless sky.
　'Some, less refined, beneath the moon's pale light
Hover, and catch the Shooting Stars by night;
Or suck the mists in grosser air below;
Or dip their pinions in the painted Bow;
Or brew fierce tempests on the wintry Main;
Or o'er the glebe distil the kindly rain.
　'Others, on Earth, o'er Human Race preside,
Watch all their ways, and all their actions guide.
Of these, the Chief the care of nations own;
And guard, with Arms divine, the British Throne.

'Our humbler province is to tend the Fair;
Not a less pleasing, though less glorious, care.
To save the powder from too rude a gale;
Nor let th' imprisoned essences exhale.
To draw fresh colours from the vernal flowers;
To steal from rainbows, ere they drop in showers,
A brighter Wash! to curl their waving hairs,
Assist their blushes, and inspire their Airs!
Nay! oft, in dreams, Invention we bestow,
To change a flounce, or add a furbelow.
  'This day, black omens threat the brightest Fair
That e'er deserved a watchful Spirit's care!
Some dire disaster, or by force, or slight;
But What, or Where, the Fates have wrapped in night!
  'Whether the Nymph shall break DIANA's law;
Or some frail china jar receive a flaw!
Or stain her honour, or her new brocade!
Forget her prayers, or miss a Masquerade!
Or lose her heart, or necklace, at a Ball!
Or whether Heaven has doomed, that Shock must fall!
  'Haste then, ye Spirits! to your charge repair!
The flutt'ring Fan be ZEPHYRETTA's care!
The Drops to thee, BRILLANTE, we consign;
And, MOMENTILLA, let the Watch be thine!
Do thou, CRISPISSA, tend her fav'rite Lock!
ARIEL himself shall be the guard of Shock!
  'To fifty chosen Sylphs of special note,
We trust th' important charge, the Petticoat!
Oft have we known that sevenfold fence to fail;
Though stiff with hoops, and armed with ribs of whale!

Alexander Pope.

Form a strong line about the silver bound,
And guard the wide circumference around!
  'Whatever Spirit, careless of his charge,
His post neglects, or leaves the Fair at large;
Shall feel sharp vengeance soon o'ertake his sins!
Be stopped in vials, or transfixed with pins,
Or plunged in lakes of bitter Washes lie,
Or wedged, whole Ages, in a bodkin's eye!
Gums and pomatums shall his flight restrain;
While, clogged, he beats his silken wings in vain!
Or alum-styptics, with contracting power,
Shrink his thin essence, like a rivelled flower!
Or, as Ixion fixed, the wretch shall feel
The giddy motion of the whirling Mill;
'Midst fumes of burning chocolate shall glow,
And tremble at the sea that froths below!'

  He spoke. The Spirits from the Sails descend.
Some, orb in orb, around the Nymph extend.
Some thread the mazy ringlets of her hair.
Some hang upon the pendants of her ear.
With beating hearts, the dire event they wait;
Anxious, and trembling for the birth of Fate.

THE RAPE OF THE LOCK.

CANTO III.

CLOSE by those meads for ever crowned with flowers,
Where Thames with pride surveys his rising towers.
There stands a structure of majestic frame,
Which from the neighb'ring Hampton takes its name.
Here, Britain's Statesmen oft the fall foredoom
Of foreign Tyrants, and of Nymphs at home!
Here, thou, great ANNA! whom three Realms obey,
Dost sometimes counsel take, and sometimes tea!

Hither, the Heroes and the Nymphs resort,
To taste awhile the pleasures of a Court!
In various talk, th' instructive hours they past,
Who gave the Ball, or paid the visit, last!
One speaks the glory of the British Queen;
And one describes a charming Indian screen.
A third interprets motions, looks, and eyes;
At ev'ry word, a reputation dies!
Snuff, or the Fan, supply each pause of chat,
With singing, laughing, ogling, and all that!

Alexander Pope.

Meanwhile, declining from the noon of day,
The sun obliquely shoots his burning ray.
The hungry Judges soon the sentence sign;
And wretches hang, that Jurymen may dine!
The merchant from th' Exchange returns in peace;
And the long labours of the Toilet cease.

BELINDA now, whom thirst of fame invites,
Burns to encounter two advent'rous Knights,
At Ombre singly, to decide their doom;
And swells her breast with conquests yet to come.
Strait, the three Bands prepare in Arms to join;
Each Band the number of the sacred Nine.
Soon as she spreads her Hand, th' aerial guard
Descend, and sit on each important card.
First, ARIEL perched upon a *Matadore*;
Then each, according to the rank they bore:
For Sylphs, yet mindful of their ancient race,
Are, as when Women, wondrous fond of Place!

Behold, four Kings in majesty revered,
With hoary whiskers and a forky beard;
And four fair Queens, whose hands sustain a flower,
Th' expressive emblem of their softer power;
Four Knaves, in garbs succinct, a trusty band,
Caps on their heads, and halberds in their hand;
And particoloured troops, a shining Train;
Draw forth, to combat on the velvet plain!

Alexander Pope.

   The skilful Nymph reviews her force with care.
'Let Spades be Trumps!' she said; and Trumps they
   Now move to war her sable *Matadores*,   [were!
In show like Leaders of the swarthy Moors.
Spadillio first, unconquerable Lord!
Led off two captive Trumps, and swept the board.
As many more *Manillio* forced to yield;
And marched a victor from the verdant Field.
Him *Basto* followed; but his fate more hard
Gained but one Trump and one plebeian card.
With his broad sabre next, a Chief in years,
The hoary Majesty of Spades appears;
Puts forth one manly leg, to sight revealed,
The rest his many-coloured robe concealed.
The rebel Knave, that dares his Prince engage,
Proves the just victim of his royal rage.
Ev'n mighty *Pam* (that Kings and Queens o'erthrew,
And mowed down armies in the fights of *Lu*),
Sad chance of war! now, destitute of aid,
Falls undistinguished by the victor Spade.

   Thus far, both armies to BELINDA yield.
Now to the Baron, Fate inclines the Field!
His warlike Amazon her host invades,
Th' Imperial Consort of the Crown of Spades!
The Club's black Tyrant first her victim died,
Spite of his haughty mien and barb'rous pride!
What boots the regal circle on his head!
His giant limbs in State unwieldy spread!

That long behind he trails his pompous robe!
And, of all Monarchs, only grasps the globe!

   The Baron now his Diamonds pours apace.
Th' embroidered King who shows but half his face,
And his refulgent Queen, with powers combined,
Of broken troops an easy conquest find!
Clubs, Diamonds, Hearts, in wild disorder seen,
With throngs promiscuous strow the level Green.
   Thus, when dispersed, a routed army runs,
Of Asia's troops, and Afric's sable sons,
With like confusion, different nations fly
In various habits, and of various dye;
The pierced battalions, disunited, fall
In heaps on heaps. One fate o'erwhelms them all!

   The Knave of Diamonds now exerts his arts,
And wins (O, shameful chance!) the Queen of Hearts.
   At this, the blood the Virgin's cheek forsook,
A livid paleness spreads o'er all her look.
She sees; and trembles at th' approaching ill!
Just in the jaws of ruin, and *Codille*!
   And now (as oft in some distempered State),
On one nice Trick depends the gen'ral fate.
An Ace of Hearts steps forth. The King unseen
Lurked in her Hand, and mourned his captive Queen.
He springs to vengeance with an eager pace;
And falls like thunder on the prostrate Ace.
   The Nymph, exulting, fills with shouts the sky;
The walls, the woods, and long canals reply!

Alexander Pope.

O, thoughtless mortals! ever blind to Fate!
Too soon dejected; and too soon elate!
Sudden, these honours shall be snatched away;
And cursed for ever, this victorious day!

For, lo! the board with cups and spoons is crowned,
The berries crackle, and the Mill goes round.
On shining altars of Japan they raise
The silver lamp, and fiery spirits blaze!
From silver spouts the grateful liquors glide;
And China's earth receives the smoking tide.
At once, they gratify their scent and taste;
While frequent cups prolong the rich repast.
Strait, hover round the Fair her airy band.
Some, as she sipped, the fuming liquor fanned;
Some o'er her lap their careful plumes displayed,
Trembling, and conscious of the rich brocade.

Coffee (which makes the Politician wise,
And see through all things with his half-shut eyes)
Sent up in vapours to the Baron's brain
New stratagems, the radiant Lock to gain.
Ah! cease, rash Youth! desist, ere 'tis too late!
Fear the just Gods, and think of Scylla's[1] fate!
Changed to a bird, and sent to flit in air;
She dearly pays for Nisus' injured hair!

[1] Vide Ovid, *Metamorphoses*, VIII.

But when to mischief mortals bend their mind;
How soon fit instruments of ill they find!
  Just then, CLARISSA drew, with tempting grace,
A two-edged weapon from her shining case.
So Ladies, in Romance, assist their Knight,
Present the spear, and arm him for the fight.
  He takes the gift with reverence, and extends
The little engine on his fingers' ends.
This, just behind BELINDA's neck he spread,
As o'er the fragrant steams she bends her head.
  Swift to the Lock, a thousand Sprights repair!
A thousand wings, by turns, blow back the hair!
And thrice they twitched the diamond in her ear;
Thrice she looked back, and thrice the foe drew near!
  Just, in that instant, anxious ARIEL sought
The close recesses of the Virgin's thought,
As, on a nosegay in her breast reclined,
He watched th' ideas rising in her mind.
Sudden, he viewed, in spite of all her art,
An earthly Lover lurking at her heart!
Amazed, confused, he found his power expired;
Resigned to Fate, and with a sigh retired.

  The Peer now spreads the glitt'ring *forfex* wide
T' inclose the Lock; now joins it, to divide!
  Ev'n then, before the fatal engine closed,
A wretched Sylph too fondly interposed!
Fate urged the shears, and cut the Sylph in twain;
But airy substance soon unites again![1]

[1] See MILTON, *Paradise Lost*, Lib. VI.

Alexander Pope.

The meeting points, the sacred hair dissever
From the fair head, for ever, and for ever!

Then flashed the living lightnings from her eyes,
And screams of horror rend th' affrighted skies!
No louder shrieks by Dames, to Heaven are cast
When husbands, or when monkeys, breathe their last;
Or when rich china vessels, fallen from high,
In glitt'ring dust and painted fragments lie!

'Let wreaths of triumph now my temples twine!'
The victor cried, 'the glorious prize is mine!
While fish, in streams, or birds delight in air,
Or in a Coach and Six, the British Fair;
As long as *Atalantis* shall be read,
Or the small pillow grace a Lady's bed;
While visits shall be paid on solemn days,
When numerous wax-lights in bright order blaze;
While Nymphs take treats, or assignations give;
So long my honour, name, and praise shall live!'

What time would spare, from steel receives its date;
And monuments, like men, submit to Fate!
Steel did the labour of the Gods destroy,
And strike to dust th' imperial towers of Troy!
Steel could the works of mortal pride confound;
And hew triumphal arches to the ground!
What wonder, then, fair Nymph! thy hairs shall feel
The conqu'ring force of unresisted steel!

Alexander Pope.

THE RAPE OF THE LOCK.

CANTO IV.

But anxious cares the pensive Nymph opprest;
And secret Passions laboured in her breast.
Not youthful Kings in battle seized alive,
Not scornful Virgins who their charms survive,
Not ardent Lovers robbed of all their bliss,
Not ancient Ladies when refused a kiss,
Not Tyrants fierce that unrepenting die,
Not CYNTHIA when her manteau 's pinned awry,
E'er felt such rage, resentment, and despair,
As thou, sad Virgin! for thy ravished hair!

For, that sad moment when the Sylphs withdrew,
And ARIEL weeping, from BELINDA flew,
UMBRIEL, a dusky melancholy Spright
As ever sullied the fair face of light,
Down to the central earth, his proper scene,
Repairs, to search the gloomy Cave of SPLEEN.

Alexander Pope.

Swift on his sooty pinions flits the Gnome,
And in a vapour reached the dismal Dome.
No cheerful breeze this sullen region knows;
The dreaded East is all the wind that blows!
Here, in a grotto, sheltered close from air,
And screened in shades from day's detested glare,
She sighs for ever, on her pensive bed;
PAIN at her side, and MEGRIM at her head.

Two handmaids wait the throne: alike in Place,
But diff'ring far in figure and in face.
Here, stood ILL NATURE, like an ancient Maid,
Her wrinkled form in black and white arrayed.
With store of Prayers for mornings, nights, and noons
Her hand is filled; her bosom, with lampoons.
There, AFFECTATION, with a sickly mien,
Shows in her cheek the roses of eighteen.
Practised to lisp, and hang the head aside,
Faints into Airs, and languishes with pride.
On the rich quilt sinks with becoming woe,
Wrapped in a gown for sickness, and for show!
The Fair Ones feel such maladies as these,
When each new night-dress gives a new disease.

A constant vapour o'er the Palace flies;
Strange phantoms rising as the mists arise,
Dreadful as Hermit's dreams in haunted shades,
Or bright as visions of expiring Maids.

Alexander Pope.

Now, glaring fiends, and snakes on rolling spires,
Pale spectres, gaping tombs, and purple fires!
Now, lakes of liquid gold, Elysian scenes,
And crystal domes, and Angels in Machines!

  Unnumbered throngs on ev'ry side are seen
Of bodies changed to various forms by SPLEEN.
Here, living Teapots stand, one arm held out,
One bent; the handle this, and that the spout.
A Pipkin there, like HOMER's Tripod[1] walks.
Here sighs a Jar; and there a Goose-pie talks!
Men prove with child, as powerful fancy works;
And maids turned Bottles, call aloud for corks!

  Safe passed the Gnome through this fantastic band,
A branch of healing Spleenwort in his hand.
Then thus addressed the Power. 'Hail, wayward Queen!
Who rule the Sex to Fifty, from Fifteen!
Parent of Vapours and of Female Wit;
Who give th' hysteric, or poetic, fit!
On various tempers act by various ways,
Make some take physic, others scribble Plays!
Who cause the Proud, their visits to delay;
And send the Godly, in a pet, to pray!
  'A Nymph there is, that all thy power disdains;
And thousands more in equal mirth maintains.
But O, if e'er thy Gnome could spoil a grace,
Or raise a pimple on a beauteous face;

---

[1] See HOMER, *Iliad*, XVIII, of VULCAN's walking Tripods.

Like Citron Waters, matrons' cheeks inflame;
Or change complexions at a losing game;
If e'er with airy horns I planted heads,
Or rumpled petticoats, or tumbled beds;
Or caused suspicion where no soul was rude,
Or discomposed the head-dress of a Prude;
Or e'er to costive lap-dog gave disease;
Which not the tears of brightest eyes could ease:
Hear me, and touch BELINDA with chagrin!
That single act gives half the World the Spleen!'

 The Goddess, with a discontented Air,
Seems to reject him; though she grants his prayer.
 A wondrous bag, with both her hands she binds,
Like that where once ULYSSES held the winds.
There she collects the force of female lungs,
Sighs, sobs, and Passions, and the war of tongues.
 A vial next she fills with fainting fears,
Soft sorrows, melting griefs, and flowing tears.
 The Gnome, rejoicing, bears her gift away;
Spreads his black wings, and slowly mounts to day.

 Sunk in THALESTRIS' arms the Nymph he found;
Her eyes dejected, and her hair unbound.
Full o'er their heads the swelling bag he rent;
And all the Furies issued at the vent!
 BELINDA burns with more than mortal ire;
And fierce THALESTRIS fans the rising fire.

'O, wretched Maid!' she spread her hands, and cried!
While Hampton's echoes 'wretched Maid!' replied,
'Was it for this, you took such constant care,
The bodkin, comb, and essence to prepare!
For this, your Locks in paper-durance bound!
For this, with tort'ring irons wreathed around!
For this, with fillets strained your tender head;
And bravely bore the double loads of lead!
 'Gods! shall the ravisher display your hair;
While the Fops envy, and the Ladies stare!
Honour forbid! at whose unrivalled shrine,
Ease, pleasure, virtue, all, our Sex resign!
 'Methinks, already, I your tears survey!
Already, hear the horrid things they say!
Already, see you a degraded Toast;
And all your honour in a whisper lost!
How shall I then, your helpless fame defend?
'Twill then, be infamy to seem your friend!
 'And shall this prize, th' inestimable prize,
Exposed through crystal to the gazing eyes,
And heightened by the diamonds' circling rays,
On that rapacious hand for ever blaze!
Sooner shall grass in Hyde Park Circus grow!
And Wits take lodgings in the sound of Bow!
Sooner let Earth, Air, Sea, to Chaos fall!
Men, monkeys, lap-dogs, parrots, perish all!'

 She said: then, raging, to Sir PLUME repairs;
And bids her Beau demand the precious hairs!

Alexander Pope.

Sir PLUME, of amber snuff-box justly vain,
And the nice conduct of a clouded cane,
With earnest eyes and round unthinking face,
He first the snuff-box opened, then the Case:
And thus broke out, 'My Lord! why, what the Devil!
Zounds! damn the Lock! 'fore Gad! you must be civil!
Plague on 't! 'Tis past a jest! Nay! prithee, pox!
Give her the hair!' He spoke, and rapped his box!

'It grieves me much,' replied the Peer again,
'Who speaks so well should ever speak in vain!
But, by this Lock![1] this sacred Lock, I swear
(Which never more shall join its parted hair!
Which never more its honours shall renew!
Clipped from the lovely head, where once it grew)
That, while my nostrils draw the vital air,
This hand, which won it, shall for ever wear!'
He spoke: in speaking, in proud triumph, spread
The long-contended honours of her head.

But UMBRIEL, hateful Gnome! forbears not so!
He breaks the vial whence the Sorrows flow!
 Then, see! The Nymph in beauteous grief appears;
Her eyes half languishing, half drowned in tears.
On her heaved bosom hung her drooping head,
Which, with a sigh, she raised; and thus she said:
 'For ever cursed be this detested day;
Which snatched my best, my fav'rite, curl away!

---

[1] In allusion to ACHILLES' oath in HOMER, *Iliad*, I.

Alexander Pope.

Happy! ah! ten times happy had I been,
If Hampton Court these eyes had never seen!
Yet am I not the first mistaken Maid,
By love of Courts to num'rous ills betrayed!
O, had I rather, unadmired, remained
In some lone isle, or distant northern land;
Where the gilt Chariot never marks the way,
Where none learn Ombre, none e'er taste Bohea!
There, kept my charms concealed from mortal eye,
Like roses that in deserts bloom and die!
 'What moved my mind with youthful Lords to roam?
O, had I stayed and said my prayers at home!
 ''Twas this, the morning omens seemed to tell!
Thrice from my trembling hand the Patch-box fell!
The tott'ring china shook without a wind!
Nay! Poll sat mute; and Shock was most unkind!
A Sylph too warned me of the threats of Fate,
In mystic visions, now believed too late!
 'See the poor remnants of these slighted hairs!
My hands shall rend what ev'n thy rapine spares!
These, in two sable ringlets taught to break,
Once gave new beauties to the snowy neck.
The sister Lock now sits uncouth, alone;
And in its fellow's fate foresees its own!
Uncurled it hangs! The fatal shears demands;
And tempts once more thy sacrilegious hands!
Oh! hadst thou, cruel! been content to seize
Hairs less in sight; or any hairs but these!'

THE RAPE OF THE LOCK.

CANTO V.

She said. The pitying audience melt in tears:
But Fate and Jove had stopped the Baron's ears!
In vain, Thalestris, with reproach assails;
For who can move, when fair Belinda fails!
Not half so fixed the Trojan could remain,
While Anna begged, and Dido urged, in vain!

[First added in the Fifth Edition of 1718.

Then grave Clarissa graceful waved her fan.
Silence ensued, and thus the Nymph began.
 'Say, why are Beauties praised and honoured most?
The wise man's Passion, and the vain man's Toast!
Why decked with all that land and sea afford?
Why Angels called, and Angel-like adored?
Why round our coaches crowd the white-gloved Beaus?
Why bows the Side-Box from its inmost rows?
 'How vain are all these glories, all our pains;
Unless Good Sense preserve what Beauty gains!
Then men may say, when we the Front-Box grace,
Behold the first in virtue, as in face!

'O, if to dance all night, and dress all day,
Charmed the Small-pox, or chased old age away;
Who would not scorn what housewife's cares produce,
Or who would learn one earthly thing of use!
To patch, nay, ogle! might become a Saint;
Nor could it, sure, be such a sin to paint!
  'But since, alas! frail Beauty must decay!
Curled, or uncurled, since Locks will turn to grey!
Since, painted, or not painted, all shall fade!
And she who scorns a Man, must die a Maid!
What then remains, but well our power to use;
And keep Good Humour still, whate'er we lose?
And trust me, Dear! Good Humour can prevail,
When Airs, and flights, and screams, and scolding fail!
Beauties, in vain, their pretty eyes may roll;
Charms strike the sight, but merit wins the soul!'

  So spake the Dame; but no applause ensued!
BELINDA frowned. THALESTRIS called her 'Prude!'
'To Arms! To Arms! the fierce virago cries;]

'To Arms! To Arms!' the bold THALESTRIS cries;
And swift as lightning to the combat flies!
  All side in Parties, and begin th' attack;
Fans clap, silks rustle, and tough whalebones crack!
Heroes' and heroines' shouts confus'dly rise;
And bass and treble voices strike the skies!
No common weapons in their hands are found;
Like Gods they fight, nor dread a mortal wound!

[1] So when bold HOMER makes the Gods engage,
And heavenly breasts with human Passions rage;
'Gainst PALLAS, MARS; LATONA, HERMES arms;
And all Olympus rings with loud alarms!
JOVE's thunder roars! Heaven trembles all around!
Blue NEPTUNE storms! The bellowing deeps resound!
Earth shakes her nodding Towers! The ground gives
And the pale ghosts start at the flash of day!   [way;

Triumphant UMBRIEL, on a sconce's height,
Clapped his glad wings; and sat to view the fight.
Propped on their bodkin spears, the Sprights survey
The growing combat; or assist the fray.

While through the press enraged THALESTRIS flies,
And scatters deaths around from both her eyes;
A Beau and Witling perished in the throng;
One died in metaphor, and one in Song.
  'O, cruel Nymph! a living death I bear!'
Cried DAPPERWIT; and sunk beside his Chair.
  A mournful glance Sir FOPLING upwards cast,
'Those eyes are made so killing!' [2] was his last.
Thus on Meander's flow'ry margin lies
Th' expiring swan; and, as he sings, he dies!

When bold Sir PLUME had drawn CLARISSA down;
CHLOE stepped in, and killed him with a frown!
She smiled to see the doughty hero slain;
But, at her smile, the Beau revived again!

[1] HOMER, *Iliad*, XX.   [2] A Song in the Opera of *Camilla*.

Alexander Pope.

[1] Now JOVE suspends his Golden Scales in air,
Weighs the men's wits against the Lady's hair;
The doubtful beam long nods from side to side.
At length, the wits mount up! the hairs subside!

See, fierce BELINDA on the Baron flies
With more than usual lightning in her eyes!
Nor feared the Chief th' unequal fight to try;
Who sought no more than on his foe to die!
But this bold Lord, with manly strength endued,
She with one finger and a thumb subdued!
Just where the breath of life his nostrils drew,
A charge of snuff the wily Virgin threw.
The Gnomes direct, to ev'ry atom just,
The pungent grains of titillating dust!
Sudden, with starting tears each eye o'erflows;
And the high dome re-echoes to his nose!

'Now, meet thy fate!' incensed BELINDA cried;
And drew a deadly bodkin from her side.
([2] The same, his ancient personage to deck,
Her great-great-grandsire wore about his neck
In three Seal-Rings; which, after, melted down
Formed a vast buckle for his Widow's gown.
Her infant grandame's whistle next it grew;
The bells she jingled, and the whistle blew.
Then in a bodkin, graced her mother's hairs;
Which long she wore, and now BELINDA wears.)

---
[1] *Vide* HOMER, *Iliad*, VIII; and VIRGIL, *Æneid*, XII.
[2] In imitation of the progress of AGAMEMNON's sceptre in HOMER, *Iliad*, II.

Alexander Pope.

'Boast not my fall!' he cried, 'insulting foe!
Thou by some other shalt be laid as low!
Nor think, to die dejects my lofty mind!
All that I dread is leaving you behind!
Rather than so, ah! let me still survive,
And burn in Cupid's flames: but burn alive!'

'Restore the Lock!' she cries; and all around
'Restore the Lock!' the vaulted roofs rebound.
Not fierce Othello, in so loud a strain,
Roared for the handkerchief that caused his pain!

But see how oft ambitious aims are crossed;
And Chiefs contend till all the prize is lost!
The Lock, obtained with guilt, and kept with pain,
In ev'ry place is sought; but sought in vain!
With such a prize no mortal must be blest!
So Heaven decrees! With Heaven, who can contest?
Some thought it mounted to the Lunar Sphere,
[1] Since all things lost on Earth are treasured there.
There, Heroes' wits are kept in pond'rous vases;
And Beaus', in snuff-boxes and tweezer cases.
There, broken vows and death-bed alms are found;
And Lovers' hearts with ends of ribband bound.
The Courtier's promises, the Sick Man's prayers,
The smiles of Harlots, and the tears of Heirs.
Cages for gnats, and chains to yoke a flea;
Dried butterflies, and tomes of Casuistry.

[1] Vide Ariosto, [*Orlando furioso*], Canto XXXIV.

Alexander Pope.

But trust the Muse! She saw it upward rise;
Though marked by none but quick poetic eyes!
(So Rome's great Founder to the Heavens withdrew;
To Procullus alone confessed in view!)
   A sudden star, it shot through liquid air;
And drew behind a radiant trail of hair!
Not Berenice's locks first rose so bright;
The heavens bespangling with dishevelled light.
   The Sylphs behold it, kindling, as it flies;
And, pleased, pursue its progress through the skies.

   This, the Beau Monde shall from the Mall survey;
And hail, with music, its propitious ray!
   This, the blessed Lover shall, for Venus take;
And send up vows from Rosamonda's Lake!
This, Partridge soon shall view in cloudless skies,
When next he looks through Galileo's eyes;
And hence, th' egregious Wizard shall foredoom
The fate of Louis, and the fall of Rome.

   Then, cease, bright Nymph! to mourn the ravished
Which adds new glory to the shining Sphere!   [hair;
Not all the tresses that fair head can boast,
Shall draw such envy as the Lock you lost!
   For, after all the murders of your eye,
When, after millions slain, yourself shall die;
When those fair suns shall set, as set they must!
And all those tresses shall be laid in dust:
This Lock, the Muse shall consecrate to Fame,
And, 'midst the stars, inscribe Belinda's name!

Alexander Pope.

THE DYING CHRISTIAN TO HIS SOUL.

[The earlier form of this imitation of the Emperor HADRIAN's *Animula, vagula, blandula,* was written in 1712, and first printed in 1730. The present is the revised text of 1736. It is thought that POPE was somewhat indebted to the poem of FLATMAN which will be found in Volume VI. 293 of this Series.]

VITAL spark of heav'nly flame;
Quit, O, quit this mortal frame!
Trembling, hoping, ling'ring, flying;
O, the pain, the bliss, of dying!
Cease, fond Nature! cease thy strife;
And let me languish into life!

Hark! they whisper! Angels say,
'Sister Spirit! come away!'
What is this absorbs me quite,
Steals my senses, shuts my sight,
Drowns my spirits, draws my breath?
Tell me, my soul! Can this be death?

The world recedes! It disappears!
Heaven opens on my eyes! My ears
  With sounds seraphic ring!
Lend, lend your wings! I mount! I fly!
O, Grave! where is thy victory?
  O, Death! where is thy sting?

Anonymous.

Here 's a Health to the Queen, and a lasting Peace!
To faction an end, to wealth increase!
Come, let 's drink it, while we have breath;
For there 's no drinking after death!
And he that will this Health deny,
Down among the dead men [*empty bottles*] let him lie!

Let charming Beauty's Health go round!
In whom celestial joys are found:
And may confusion still pursue
The senseless woman-hating crew!
And they that Woman's Health deny,
Down among the dead men let them lie!

In smiling BACCHUS' joys I'll roll!
Deny no pleasure to my soul!
Let BACCHUS' Health, round briskly move;
For BACCHUS is a friend to Love!
And he that will his Health deny,
Down among the dead men let him lie!

May Love and Wine, their rites maintain;
And their united pleasures reign!
While BACCHUS' treasure crowns the board;
We'll sing the joys that both afford!
And they that won't with us comply,
Down among the dead men let them lie!

Rt. Hon. Joseph Addison.

A LETTER FROM ITALY

TO THE RT. HON. CHARLES MONTAGU, LORD HALIFAX,

1701.

Salve magna parens frugum Saturnia tellus,
Magna Virum! tibi res antiquæ laudis et artis
Aggredior, sanctos ausus recludere fontes.

VIRGIL, *Georgics*, II.

WHILE you, my Lord! the rural shades admire,
And from BRITANNIA's Public Posts retire;
Nor longer, her ungrateful sons to please,
For their advantage, sacrifice your ease:
Me into foreign realms my fate conveys,
Through nations fruitful of immortal Lays;
Where the soft season and inviting clime
Conspire to trouble your repose with rhyme.

For wheresoe'er I turn my ravished eyes,
Gay gilded scenes and shining prospects rise!

Rt. Hon. Joseph Addison.

Poetic fields encompass me around;
And still I seem to tread on classic ground!
For here, the Muse so oft her harp has strung,
That not a mountain rears its head unsung!
Renowned in Verse each shady thicket grows,
And ev'ry stream in heavenly Numbers flows!

How am I pleased to search the hills and woods
For rising springs and celebrated floods!
To view the Nar, tumultuous in his course;
And trace the smooth Clitumnus to his source!
To see the Mincio draw his wat'ry store
Through the long windings of a fruitful shore;
And hoary Albula's infected tide,
O'er the warm bed of smoking sulphur glide!

Fired with a thousand raptures, I survey
Eridanus through flow'ry meadows stray!
The King of Floods! that, rolling o'er the plains,
The tow'ring Alps of half their moisture drains;
And, proudly swollen with a whole Winter's snows,
Distributes wealth and plenty where he flows!

Sometimes, misguided by the tuneful throng,
I look for streams immortalized in Song,
That lost in silence and oblivion lie
(Dumb are their fountains, and their channels dry):
Yet run for ever, by the Muses' skill;
And in the smooth description murmur still!

Sometimes, to gentle Tiber I retire,
And the famed river's empty shores admire;
That, destitute of strength, derives its course
From thrifty urns and an unfruitful source:
Yet, sung so often in poetic Lays,
With scorn the Danube and the Nile surveys!
So high the deathless Muse exalts her theme!
  Such was the Boyne! a poor inglorious stream
That in Hibernian vales obscurely strayed,
And unobserved in wild meanders played,
Till by *your* lines and NASSAU's sword renowned,
Its rising billows through the World resound,
Where'er the Hero's Godlike acts can pierce;
Or where the fame of an immortal Verse!

  O, could the Muse, my ravished breast inspire
With warmth like yours, and raise an equal fire;
Unnumbered beauties in my Verse should shine,
And VIRGIL's Italy should yield to mine!

  See, how the golden groves around me smile!
That shun the coast of Britain's stormy isle:
Or, when transplanted and preserved with care,
Curse the cold clime; and starve in northern air!
Here, kindly warmth their mounting juice ferments
To nobler tastes, and more exalted scents!
Ev'n the rough rocks with tender myrtle bloom;
And trodden weeds send out a rich perfume!
  Bear me, some God! to Baja's gentle seats;
Or cover me in Umbria's green retreats!

Rt. Hon. Joseph Addison.

Where western gales eternally reside,
And all the Seasons lavish all their pride.
Blossoms, and fruits, and flowers together rise;
And the whole year, in gay confusion lies!

   Immortal glories in my mind revive,
And in my soul a thousand Passions strive,
When Rome's exalted beauties I descry
Magnificent in piles of ruin lie.
An Amphitheatre's amazing height
Here fills my eye with terror and delight!
That, on its Public Shows, unpeopled Rome;
And held uncrowded nations in its womb!
Here, pillars rough with sculpture pierce the skies;
And here, the proud Triumphal Arches rise:
Where the old Romans' deathless acts displayed,
Their base degenerate progeny upbraid!
Whole rivers here, forsake the fields below;
And, wond'ring at their height, through airy channels
     flow!

   Still to new scenes my wand'ring Muse retires,
And the dumb show of breathing rocks admires:
Where the smooth chisel all its force has shown,
And softened into flesh the rugged stone!
In solemn silence, a majestic band,
Heroes, and Gods, and Roman Consuls, stand.
Stern tyrants, whom their cruelties renown,
And Emperors, in Parian marble frown;

While the bright Dames, to whom they humbly sued,
Still show the charms that their proud hearts subdued.

   Fain would I RAPHAEL's Godlike art rehearse;
And show th' immortal labours in my Verse!
Where, from the mingled strength of shade and light,
A new creation rises to my sight!
Such heavenly figures from his pencil flow,
So warm with life his blended colours glow,
From theme to theme with secret pleasure tost,
Amidst the soft variety I'm lost!
   Here, pleasing Airs my ravished soul confound
With circling notes and labyrinths of sound!
   Here, Domes and Temples rise in distant views;
And opening Palaces invite my Muse!

   How has kind Heaven adorned the happy land;
And scattered blessings with a wasteful hand!
But what avail her unexhausted stores,
Her blooming mountains, and her sunny shores;
With all the gifts that Heaven and Earth impart,
The smiles of Nature, and the charms of Art;
While proud Oppression in her valleys reigns,
And Tyranny usurps her happy plains?
   The poor inhabitant beholds in vain
The redd'ning orange and the swelling grain;
Joyless he sees the growing oils and wines,
And in the myrtle's fragrant shade repines;
Starves in the midst of Nature's bounty curst,
And in the loaden vineyard dies for thirst!

Rt. Hon. Joseph Addison.

O, LIBERTY! thou Goddess heavenly bright!
Profuse of bliss, and pregnant with delight!
Eternal pleasures in thy presence reign;
And smiling Plenty leads thy wanton Train!
Eased of her load, Subjection grows more light;
And Poverty looks cheerful in thy sight!
Thou mak'st the gloomy face of Nature gay;
Giv'st beauty to the sun, and pleasure to the day!

Thee, Goddess! Thee, BRITANNIA's Isle adores!
How has she oft exhausted all her stores!
How oft, in Fields of Death, thy presence sought;
Nor thinks the mighty prize too dearly bought!

On foreign mountains may the sun refine
The grape's soft juice, and mellow it to wine!
With citron groves adorn a distant soil;
And the fat olive swell with floods of oil!
We envy not the warmer clime that lies
In ten degrees of more indulgent skies;
Nor at the coarseness of our heaven repine,
Though o'er our heads the frozen Pleiads shine:
'Tis Liberty that crowns BRITANNIA's Isle,
And makes her barren rocks and her bleak mountains
    smile!

Others with tow'ring Piles may please the sight;
And in their proud aspiring Domes delight!
A nicer touch to the stretched canvas give;
Or teach their animated rocks to live!

Rt. Hon. Joseph Addison.

'Tis Britain's care to watch o'er Europe's fate;
And hold in balance each contending State!
To threaten bold presumptuous Kings with war;
And answer her afflicted neighbours' prayer!
The Dane and Swede, roused up by fierce alarms,
Bless the wise conduct of her pious Arms!
Soon as her Fleets appear, their terrors cease;
And all the Northern World lies hushed in peace!

Th' ambitious Gaul beholds, with secret dread,
Her thunder aimed at his aspiring head;
And fain her Godlike sons would disunite
By foreign gold, or by domestic spite:
But strives in vain to conquer, or divide;
Whom Nassau's Arms defend, and counsels guide!

Fired with the name, while I so oft have found
The distant climes and different tongues resound,
I bridle in my struggling Muse with pain!
That longs to launch into a bolder strain.

But I've already troubled you too long;
Nor dare attempt a more advent'rous Song;
My humble Verse demands a softer theme,
A painted meadow, or a purling stream!
Unfit for Heroes! whom immortal Lays,
And lines like Virgil's, or like yours, should praise!

Rt. Hon. Joseph Addison.

SONGS FROM 'ROSAMOND.'

BENEATH some hoary mountain,
  I'll lay me down and weep!
Or near some warbling fountain,
  Bewail myself asleep!
Where feathered quires combining
  With gentle murmuring streams,
And winds in consort joining,
  Raise sadly-pleasing dreams.

O, THE pleasing, pleasing anguish!
When we love, and when we languish!
    Wishes rising!
    Thoughts surprising!
    Pleasure courting!
    Charms transporting!
    Fancy viewing
    Joys ensuing!
O, the pleasing, pleasing anguish!

IF 'tis joy to wound a Lover,
  How much more to give him ease!
When his Passion we discover,
  O, how pleasing 'tis to please!
    The bliss returns; and we receive
    Transports greater than we give!

Alexander Pope.

PROLOGUE

TO ADDISON'S TRAGEDY OF 'CATO.'
1713.

To wake the Soul, by tender strokes of Art!
To raise the genius, and to mend the heart!
To make Mankind, in conscious virtue bold,
Live o'er each scene, and Be what they behold!
For this, the Tragic Muse first trod the Stage,
Commanding tears to stream through every Age.
Tyrants no more their savage nature kept;
And foes to Virtue wondered how they wept!
  Our Author shuns, by vulgar springs, to move
The Hero's glory, or the Virgin's love!
In pitying Love, we but our weakness show;
And wild Ambition well deserves its woe!
  Here, tears shall flow from a more gen'rous cause;
Such tears as Patriots shed for dying Laws!
He bids your breasts with ancient ardour rise;
And calls forth Roman drops from British eyes!
Virtue confessed in human shape he draws;
What PLATO thought, and Godlike CATO was!
No common object to your sight displays;
But what, with pleasure Heaven itself surveys:

Alexander Pope.

A brave man struggling in the storms of Fate;
And greatly falling, with a falling State!
While CATO gives his little Senate laws;
What bosom beats not in his country's cause!
Who sees him act; but envies every deed!
Who hears him groan; and does not wish to bleed!
 Even when proud CÆSAR, 'midst triumphal cars,
The spoils of nations, and the pomp of wars,
Ignobly vain, and impotently great,
Showed Rome, her CATO's figure drawn in State;
As her dead Father's reverend image past,
The pomp was darkened, and the day o'ercast!
The Triumph ceased! Tears gushed from every eye!
The World's great Victor passed unheeded by!
Her last good man, dejected Rome adored;
And honoured CÆSAR's, less than CATO's, sword!

 Britons, attend! Be worth like this approved;
And shew you have the virtue to be moved!
With honest scorn, the first famed CATO viewed
Rome learning arts from Greece; whom she subdued.
Our Scene precariously subsists too long
On French Translation, and Italian Song!
Dare to have sense yourselves! Assert the Stage!
Be justly warmed with your own native rage!
Such Plays alone should please a British ear,
As CATO's self had not disdained to hear.

Rt. Hon. Joseph Addison.

THE SOLILOQUY OF CATO.

CATO, solus, sitting in a thoughtful posture. In his hand, PLATO's book on The Immortality of the Soul. *A drawn sword on a table by him.*

IT must be so! PLATO, thou reason'st well!
Else whence this pleasing hope, this fond desire,
This longing after Immortality!
Or whence this secret dread and inward horror
Of falling into nought! Why shrinks the Soul
Back on herself; and startles at destruction?
'Tis the divinity that stirs within us!
'Tis Heaven itself, that points out an Hereafter;
And intimates Eternity to Man!
   Eternity! thou pleasing, dreadful thought!
Through what variety of untried Being,
Through what new scenes and changes, must we pass!
The wide, th' unbounded, prospect lies before me;
But shadows, clouds, and darkness rest upon it!
   Here, will I hold! If there 's a Power above us
(And that there is, all Nature cries aloud

Rt. Hon. Joseph Addison.

Through all her works!), he must delight in virtue!
And that which he delights in, must be happy!
But when? or where? This world was made for
    Cæsar!
I'm weary of conjectures! This must end them!
                         [*Laying his hand on his sword.*

    Thus am I doubly armed! My death and life,
My bane and antidote, are both before me!
This, in a moment, brings me to an end;
But this informs me, I shall never die!
The Soul, secured in her existence, smiles
At the drawn dagger, and defies its point!
The stars shall fade away, the sun himself
Grow dim with age, and Nature sink in years:
But thou shalt flourish in immortal youth;
Unhurt amidst the war of Elements,
The wrecks of Matter, and the crush of Worlds!

    What means this heaviness, that hangs upon me?
This lethargy, that creeps through all my senses?
Nature, oppressed and harassed out with care,
Sinks down to rest. This once, I'll favour her!
That my awakened Soul may take her flight,
Renewed in all her strength, and fresh with life,
An off'ring fit for Heaven! Let guilt, or fear,
Disturb Man's rest: Cato knows neither of them!
Indiff'rent in his choice, to sleep, or die.

Mary, Lady Chudleigh.

Why, Damon! why, why, why so pressing?
The heart you beg 's not worth possessing!
Each look, each word, each smile, 's affected;
And inward charms are quite neglected!
Then scorn her! scorn her! foolish Swain;
And sigh no more, no more in vain!

Beauty 's worthless! fading! flying!
Who would, for trifles, think of dying?
Who, for a face, a shape, would languish;
And tell the brooks and groves his anguish,
Till She, till She thinks fit to prize him;
And all, and all beside, despise him?

Fix, fix your thoughts on what 's inviting!
On what will never bear the slighting!
Wit and Virtue claim your duty!
They're much more worth than Gold and Beauty!
To them, to them, your heart resign;
And you'll no more, no more repine!

When Daphne first her Shepherd saw;
  A sudden trembling seized her!
Honour, her wond'ring looks did awe;
  She durst not view what pleased her!

When, at her feet, he sighing lay,
    She found her heart complying;
Yet would not to her love give way,
    To save her Swain from dying!

The little God stood laughing by,
    To see her dext'rous feigning.
He bid the blushing Fair comply!
    The Shepherd leave complaining!

DAMON.   Cease, fair CALISTRIS! cease disdaining!
    'Tis time to leave that useless art!
    Your Shepherd 's weary of complaining!
    Be kind; or he'll resume his heart!

CALISTRIS. *DAMON, be gone! I hate complying!*
    Go, court some fond, believing Maid!
    I take more pleasure in denying,
    Than in the conquests I have made!

DAMON.   Why, cruel Nymph! why, why so slighting?
    Is this the treatment I must have?
    Were not your beauty so inviting,
    I would no longer be your slave!

CALISTRIS. *DAMON, be gone! I hate complying!*
    Your heart 's not worth the having!
    Were there ten thousand Shepherds dying;
    Not one were worth the saving!

William Walsh.

Of all the torments, all the cares,
  With which our lives are curst;
Of all the plagues a Lover bears,
  Sure, Rivals are the worst!
By partners, in each other kind,
  Afflictions easier grow!
In Love alone, we hate to find
  Companions of our woe!

Sylvia! for all the pangs you see
  Are lab'ring in my breast,
I beg not you would favour me;
  Would you but slight the rest!
How great soe'er your rigours are;
  With them alone, I'll cope!
I can endure my own despair;
  But not another's hope!

THE DESPAIRING LOVER.

Distracted with care
For Phillis the fair,
  Since nothing could move her,
  Poor Damon, her Lover,
Resolves, in despair,
  No longer to languish,
  Nor bear so much anguish!

But, mad with his love,
   To a precipice goes;
Where a leap from above
   Would soon finish his woes!

When, in rage, he came there,
   Beholding how steep
The sides did appear,
   And the bottom how deep!
His torments projecting,
And sadly reflecting
That a Lover forsaken,
   A new Love may get;
But a neck, when once broken,
   Can never be set!
And that he could die
   Whenever he would;
But that he could live
   But as long as he could!
How grievous soever
   The torment might grow;
He scorned to endeavour
   To finish it so!

But bold, unconcerned
   At thoughts of the pain,
He calmly returned
   To his cottage again.

'Cupid! instruct an am'rous Swain,
Some way to tell the Nymph his pain,
  To common Youths unknown!
To talk of Sighs, of Flames, and Darts,
Of bleeding Wounds, and burning Hearts,
  Are methods vulgar grown!'

'What need'st thou tell?' the God replied,
'That love the Shepherd cannot hide,
  The Nymph will quickly find!
When Phœbus does his beams display
To tell men gravely "That 'tis day!"
  Is to suppose them blind!'

PHILLIS'S RESOLUTION.

'When Slaves their liberty require,
  They hope no more to gain!
But you, not only *that* require;
  But ask the power to reign!

'Think how unjust a suit you make;
  Then you will soon decline!
Your freedom, when you please, pray, take;
  But trespass not on mine!

'No more, in vain, Alcander! crave!
  I ne'er will grant the thing!
That he, who once has been my Slave,
  Should ever be my King!'

John Glanvill.

IPHIS AND IANTHE.

IANTHE the lovely, the joy of her Swain,
By IPHIS was loved; and loved IPHIS again!
She lived in the Youth; and the Youth, in the Fair!
Their pleasure was equal, and equal their care!
No time, no enjoyment, the dotage withdrew;
But the longer they loved, still the fonder they grew!

A Passion so happy alarmed all the plain.
Some envied the Nymph; but more envied the Swain!
Some swore, 'Twould be pity, their loves to invade;
That the Lovers alone for each other were made!
But all, all, consented, That none ever knew
A Nymph yet so kind; or a Shepherd so true!

LOVE saw them with pleasure; and vowed to take care
Of the faithful, the tender, the innocent pair!
What either did want, he bid either to move;
But they wanted nothing but ever to love!
Said, 'Twas all that to bless them, his Godhead could do,
If they still might be kind, and they still might be true!

William Congreve.

TO A CANDLE.

Thou watchful Taper, by whose silent light
I lonely pass the melancholy night!
Thou faithful witness of my secret pain;
To whom alone I venture to complain!
O, learn with me, my hopeless love to moan!
Commiserate a life so like thy own!
　Like thine, my flames to my destruction turn;
Wasting that heart, by which supplied they burn!
Like thine, my joy and suffering they display;
At once, are signs of life, and symptoms of decay!
　And as thy fearful flames the day decline,
And only, during night, presume to shine;
Their humble rays not daring to aspire
Before the sun, the fountain of their fire:
So mine, with conscious shame and equal awe,
To shades obscure and solitude withdraw!
Nor dare their light before her eyes disclose;
From whose bright beams their Being first arose.

　　Thus to a ripe, consenting Maid,
　　Poor, old, repenting Delia said,
　　'Would you long preserve your Lover?
　　　Would you still his Goddess reign?
　　Never let him all discover!
　　　Never let him much obtain!

William Congreve.

'Men will admire, adore, and die;
While, wishing, at your feet they lie!
But admitting their embraces
   Wakes them from the golden dream!
Nothing 's new, besides our faces!
   Every woman is the same!'

———

SEE! see, she wakes! SABINA wakes!
   And, now, the sun begins to rise!
Less glorious is the Morn that breaks
   From his bright beams, than her fair eyes!

With light united, day they give;
   But different fates, ere night fulfil!
How many, by his warmth, will live!
   How many will her coldness kill!

———

FALSE though She be to me and Love;
   I'll ne'er pursue revenge!
For still the Charmer I approve;
   Though I deplore her change!

In hours of bliss, we oft have met;
   They could not always last!
And though the present I regret;
   I'm grateful for the past!

SEMELE TO JUPITER.

With my frailty, don't upbraid me!
I am Woman, as you made me!
Causeless doubting, or despairing;
Rashly trusting, idly fearing;
  If obtaining,
   Still complaining;
  If consenting,
   Still repenting;
  Most complying,
   When denying;
And to be followed, only flying.

With my frailty, don't upbraid me!
I am Woman, as you made me!

———

I looked, and I sighed, and I wished I could speak;
 And very fain would have been at her:
But when I strove most, my Passion to break;
 Still then I said least of the matter!

I swore to myself, and resolved I would try
 Some way, my poor heart to recover;
But that was all vain! for I sooner could die,
 Than live with forbearing to love her!

Dear Cœlia! be kind then! and since your own eyes
  By looks can command adoration;
Give mine leave to talk too, and do not despise
  Those oglings that tell you my Passion!

We'll look, and we'll love! and though neither should
      speak,
  The pleasure we'll still be pursuing!
And so, without words, I don't doubt we may make
  A very good end of this wooing!

THE PETITION.

'Grant me, gentle Love,' said I,
'One dear blessing ere I die!
Long I've borne excess of pain;
Let me now some bliss obtain!'

Thus to almighty Love I cried;
When, angry, thus the God replied.
'Blessings greater none can have!
Art thou not Amynta's slave?
Cease, fond mortal! to implore;
For Love, Love himself, 's no more!'

William Congreve.

A HUE AND CRY
AFTER FAIR AMORET.

Fair Amoret is gone astray!
   Pursue and seek her, ev'ry Lover!
I'll tell the signs, by which you may
   The wand'ring Shepherdess discover!

Coquet and coy at once her Air,
   Both studied; though both seem neglected!
Careless she is, with artful care;
   Affecting to seem unaffected!

With skill, her eyes dart ev'ry glance;
   Yet change so soon, you'd ne'er suspect them!
For she'd persuade, they wound by chance;
   Though certain aim and art direct them!

She likes herself; yet others hates
   For that which in herself she prizes!
And, while she laughs at them, forgets
   She is the thing that she despises!

Thomas Ellwood.

LOVE'S ORIGINAL.

    Love is a scion cropped from Virtue's tree,
And grafted in the stock of Purity;
Planted at first in Nature's choicest soil,
Before the Fiend did Nature's beauty spoil:
But thence transplanted to a richer ground
Than can in all Dame Nature's realm be found;
Where, being well manured, it takes deep root
Downward, and branches upward forth doth shoot.
    The sap, which doth this stately tree maintain,
Is Sympathy: which runs, as in a vein,
Through every branch; causing it first to sprout,
And ere awhile, young tender buds spring out!
    Nor is it barren; but much fruit doth bear,
To taste most pleasing, and to sight most fair:
A sound substantial fruit that can endure
The sharpest frost, and yet continue pure.
And that ye may this fruit the more admire,
Take notice, that I call it Chaste Desire!

Captain Sir Richard Steele.

Why, lovely Charmer! tell me, Why
So very kind; and yet so shy?
Why does that cold forbidding Air
Give damps of sorrow and despair?
Or why that smile, my soul subdue;
And kindle up my flames anew?

In vain, you strive, with all your art,
By turns, to freeze, and fire, my heart!
When I behold a face so fair,
So sweet a look, so soft an Air;
My ravished soul is charmed all o'er!
I cannot love thee less, or more!

Let not Love on me bestow
Soft distress, and tender woe!
I know none but substantial blisses,
Eager glances, solid kisses!
I know not what the Lovers feign
Of finer pleasure mixed with pain!
Then, prithee, give me, gentle Boy!
None of thy grief; but all thy joy!

While gentle Parthenissa walks,
And sweetly smiles, and gaily talks;
A thousand shafts around her fly!
A thousand Swains, unheeded, die!

Captain Sir Richard Steele.

If then, she labours to be seen
With all her killing Air and mien;
From so much beauty, so much art,
What mortal can secure his heart!

THE DISTRESS OF A LOVE-SICK MAID.

FROM place to place forlorn I go,
  With downcast eyes, a silent shade!
Forbidden to declare my woe;
  To speak till spoken to, afraid!

My inward pangs, my secret grief,
  My soft consenting looks betray!
He loves; but gives me no relief!
  Why speaks not he, who may?

ME CUPID made a happy slave;
  A merry wretched man!
I slight the Nymphs I cannot have!
  Nor dote on those I can!

This constant maxim still I hold,
  To baffle all despair,
The absent, ugly are and old;
  The present, young and fair.

George Farquhar.

A TRIFLING Song you shall hear;
   Begun with a trifle and ended.
All trifling people, draw near;
   And I shall be nobly attended!

Were it not for trifles a few,
   That lately have come into play;
The men would want something to do,
   And the women want something to say!

What makes men trifle in dressing?
   Because the Ladies, they know,
Admire, by often possessing,
   That eminent trifle, a Beau! . . .

What mortal man would be able
   At WHITE's half an hour to sit,
Or who could bear a tea-table;
   Without talking of trifles for wit!

The Court is from trifles secure!
   Gold Keys are no trifles, we see!
White Rods are no trifles, I'm sure;
   Whatever their bearers may be!

But if you will go to the place
   Where trifles abundantly breed,
The Levée will show you his Grace
   Makes promises trifles indeed!

George Farquhar.

A coach with six footmen behind,
   I count neither trifle, nor sin;
But, ye Gods! how oft do we find
   A scandalous trifle within!

A flask of Champagne, people think it
   A trifle, or something as bad;
But if you'll contrive how to drink it,
   You'll find it no trifle, egad!

A Parson 's a trifle at sea!
   A Widow 's a trifle in sorrow!
A Peace is a trifle to-day;
   Who knows what may happen to-morrow?

A Black Coat, a trifle may cloak;
   Or to hide it, the Red may endeavour!
But if once the Army is broke;
   We shall have more trifles than ever!

The Stage is a trifle, they say;
   The reason, pray carry along!
Because, at ev'ry new Play,
   The House they with trifles so throng.

But with people's malice to trifle,
   And to set us all on a foot;
The Author of this is a trifle;
   And his Song is a trifle to boot!

Pierre Antoine Motteux.

LOVE AND FOLLY.

A FABLE.

Love and Folly were at play,
  Both too wanton to be wise.
They fell out; and, in the fray,
  Folly put out Cupid's eyes.
Straight, the criminal was tried,
  And this punishment assigned.
Folly should to Love be tied,
  And condemned to lead the blind.
Then, wisely let 's venture ourselves to deceive,
Since Fate has decreed us to love and believe!
For all we can gain, by our wisdom and eyes,
Is to find ourselves cheated; and wretched, when wise!

Pierre Antoine Motteux.

SECRET LOVE.

I love! but She alone shall know;
   Who is herself my treasure!
Vain Lovers, when their joys they show,
   Call partners to their pleasure!
Let empty Beaus the favour miss,
   While they would have it known!
That Soul's too narrow for the bliss;
   Who can't enjoy alone!

Then, never let my love be told
   By way of modern Toasting!
The sweetest joy, like fairy gold,
   Is lost by selfish boasting!
Too rich to shew what I possess,
   My treasure I'll conceal!
I may my pains of Love confess;
   But ne'er my joys reveal!

LOVE DISARMED.

Beneath a myrtle's verdant shade,
As Cloe, half asleep, was laid,
Cupid perched lightly on her breast,
And in that heaven desired to rest:
Over her paps, his wings he spread;
Between, he found a downy bed,
And nestled in his little head.

Still lay the God. The Nymph, surprised,
Yet mistress of herself, devised
How she the Vagrant might inthrall,
And captive him who captives all!

Her bodice half way she unlaced;
About his arms she slily cast
The silken bond, and held him fast.

The God awaked; and thrice, in vain,
He strove to break the cruel chain!
And thrice, in vain, he shook his wing,
Incumbered in the silken string!
Flutt'ring, the God, and weeping, said,
  'Pity poor Cupid, generous Maid!

Matthew Prior.

Who happened, being blind, to stray;
And on thy bosom lost his way!
Who strayed, alas! but knew too well
He never there must hope to dwell!
Set an unhappy pris'ner free;
Who ne'er intended harm to thee!'

'To me pertains not,' she replies,
'To know, or care, where CUPID flies!
What are his haunts, or which his way!
Where he would dwell, or whither stray!
Yet will I never set thee free;
For harm was meant, and meant to me!'

'Vain fears that vex thy virgin heart!
I'll give thee up my bow and dart;
Untangle but this cruel chain,
And freely let me fly again!'

'Agreed! Secure my virgin heart!
Instant give up thy bow and dart!
The chain I'll in return untie,
And freely thou again shalt fly!'

Thus she the captive did deliver;
The captive thus gave up his quiver!

Matthew Prior.

The God disarmed, e'er since that day,
Passes his life in harmless play;
Flies round, or sits upon her breast,
A little, flutt'ring, idle guest!

E'er since that day, the beauteous Maid
Governs the World in CUPID's stead:
Directs his arrow as she wills;
Gives grief, or pleasure! spares, or kills!

IN vain, you tell your parting Lover,
You wish fair winds may waft him over!
Alas! what winds can happy prove,
That bear me far from what I love?
Alas! what dangers on the Main
Can equal those that I sustain
From slighted vows, and cold disdain?

Be gentle! and, in pity, choose
To wish the wildest tempests loose!
That, thrown again upon the coast
Where first my shipwracked heart was lost,
I may, once more, repeat my pain!
Once more, in dying notes complain
Of slighted vows, and cold disdain!

CUPID AND GANYMEDE.

In Heaven, one holiday, you read
In wise ANACREON, GANYMEDE
Drew heedless CUPID in, to throw
A Main, to pass an hour or so.
The little Trojan, by the way,
By HERMES taught, played all the play!

The God, unhappily engaged,
By nature rash, by Play enraged,
Complained, and sighed, and cried, and fretted,
Lost ev'ry earthly thing he betted!
In ready money, all the store
Picked up, long since, from DANÆ's Shower!
A Snush-box set with bleeding hearts,
Rubies, all pierced with diamond darts!
His Nine-pins, made of myrtle wood;
The tree in Ida's forest stood!
His Bowl pure gold, the very same
Which PARIS gave the Cyprian Dame!
Two Table-Books, in shagreen covers,
Filled with good verse from real Lovers;
Merchandise rare! A *Billet-doux*,
Its matter passionate; yet true!
Heaps of Hair Rings, and Cyphered Seals!
Rich trifles! serious bagatelles!

Matthew Prior.

    What sad disorders Play begets!
Desp'rate and mad, at length, he sets
Those darts; whose points make Gods adore
His might, and deprecate his power!
Those darts; whence all our joy and pain
Arise! Those darts—'Come, Seven 's the Main!'
Cries GANYMEDE. The usual trick!
'Seven, slur a Six, Eleven! A nick!'

    Ill news goes fast! 'Twas quickly known,
That simple CUPID was undone!
    Swifter than lightning VENUS flew!
Too late she found the thing too true!
Guess how the Goddess greets her son!
    'Come hither, Sirrah! No! begone!
And, hark ye! is it so indeed?
A comrade you, for GANYMEDE!
An imp as wicked, for his age,
As any earthly Lady's Page!
A scandal and a scourge to Troy!
A Prince's son! A blackguard boy!
A sharper that, with box and dice,
Draws in young Deities to vice!

    'All Heaven is by the ears together,
Since first that little rogue came hither!
JUNO herself has had no peace;
And, truly, I've been favoured less!
For JOVE, as FAME reports (but FAME
Says things not fit for me to name!),

Has acted ill, for such a God;
And taken ways extremely odd!

'And thou, unhappy child!' she said,
(Her anger by her grief allayed)
'Unhappy child! who thus hast lost
All the estate we e'er could boast!
Whither? O, whither wilt thou run;
Thy name despised, thy weakness known?
Nor shall thy shrine on Earth be crowned,
Nor shall thy power in Heaven be owned;
When thou, nor Man, nor God, canst wound!'

Obedient CUPID, kneeling, cried,
'Cease, dearest Mother! cease to chide!
GANY's a Cheat; and I'm a Bubble!
Yet why this great excess of trouble?
The dice were false! the darts are gone!
Yet how are you, or I, undone?
The loss of these I can supply
With keener darts from CLOE's eye!
Fear not, we e'er can be disgraced
While that bright magazine shall last!
Your crowded altars still shall smoke;
And Man, your friendly aid invoke!
JOVE shall again revere your power;
And rise a Swan, or fall a Shower!'

Matthew Prior.

THE DESPAIRING SHEPHERD.

ALEXIS shunned his fellow Swains,
Their rural sports, and jovial strains.
  (Heaven guard us all from CUPID's bow!)
He lost his crook. He left his flocks;
And, wand'ring through the lonely rocks,
  He nourished endless woe!

The Nymphs and Shepherds round him came:
His grief, some pity! others blame!
  The fatal cause all kindly seek.
He mingled his concern with theirs;
He gave them back their friendly tears;
  He sighed; but would not speak!

CLORINDA came, among the rest;
And she too kind concern exprest,
  And asked the reason of his woe.
She asked: but with an Air and mien
That made it easily foreseen,
  She feared too much to know.

The Shepherd raised his mournful head,
'And will you pardon me,' he said,
  'While I, the cruel truth reveal?
Which nothing from my breast should tear,
Which never should offend your ear,
  But that you bid me tell.

"'Tis thus I rove, 'tis thus complain;
Since you appeared upon the plain!
　You are the cause of all my care!
Your eyes, ten thousand dangers dart!
Ten thousand torments vex my heart!
　I love, and I despair!'

'Too much, ALEXIS! I have heard!
'Tis what I thought! 'tis what I feared!
　And yet I pardon you!' she cried,
'But you must promise ne'er again
To breathe your vows; or speak your pain!'
　He bowed, obeyed, and died!

A DUTCH PROVERB.

'FIRE, Water, Woman, are Man's ruin!'
Says wise Professor VAN DER BRUIN.
By flames, a house I hired was lost
Last year; and I must pay the cost!
This Spring, the rains o'erflowed my ground;
And my best Flanders mare was drowned!
A slave I am to CLARA's eyes;
The gipsy knows her power, and flies!
Fire, Water, Woman, are my ruin;
And great thy wisdom, VAN DER BRUIN!

Matthew Prior.

TO A CHILD OF QUALITY, OF FIVE YEARS OLD; THE AUTHOR SUPPOSED, FORTY.

LORDS, Knights, and Squires, the num'rous Band
    That wear the fair Miss MARY's fetters,
Were summoned, by her high command,
    To show their Passion by their Letters.

My pen, amongst the rest, I took,
    Lest those bright eyes, that cannot read,
Should dart their kindling fires; and look
    The power they have to be obeyed.

Nor Quality, nor Reputation,
    Forbid me yet my flame to tell!
Dear Five Years Old befriends my Passion!
    And I may write till she can spell!

For, while she makes her silk-worms beds
    With all the tender things I swear;
Whilst all the house, my Passion reads,
    In papers round her baby's hair;

She may receive, and own my flame!
    For, though the strictest Prudes should know it,
She'll pass for a most virtuous Dame;
    And I, for an unhappy Poet!

Then too, alas! when she shall tear
  The lines some younger Rival sends,
She'll give me leave to write, I fear;
  And we shall still continue friends!

For as our diff'rent ages move,
  'Tis so ordained, (Would Fate but mend it!)
That I shall be past making love,
  When she begins to comprehend it.

While from our looks, fair Nymph! you guess
  The secret Passions of our mind,
'My heavy eyes,' you say, 'confess
  A heart to Love and Grief inclined!'

There needs, alas! but little art
  To have this fatal secret found!
With the same ease you threw the dart,
  'Tis certain, you may show the wound!

How can I see you, and not love?
  While you, as opening East are fair!
While cold as northern blasts you prove;
  How can I love, and not despair?

The wretch, in double fetters bound,
  Your potent mercy may release!
Soon, if my love by you were crowned,
  Fair Prophetess! my grief would cease!

Matthew Prior.

THE QUESTION TO LISETTA.

   What Nymph should I admire, or trust,
But Cloe beauteous! Cloe just?
   What Nymph should I desire to see,
But her who leaves the plain for me?
   To whom should I compose the Lay,
But her who listens when I play?
   To whom, in Song repeat my cares,
But her who in my sorrow shares?
   For whom should I the garland make,
But her who joys the gift to take,
And boasts she wears it for my sake?
   In love, am I not fully blest?
Lisetta, prithee, tell the rest!

LISETTA'S REPLY.

   Sure, Cloe just, and Cloe fair,
Deserves to be your only care!
But (when you and she, to-day,
Far into the wood did stray;
And I happened to pass by)
Which way did you cast your eye?
   But when your cares to her you sing;
You dare not tell her, whence they spring!
Does it not more afflict your heart,
That in those cares she bears a part?

Matthew Prior.

When you the flowers for CLOE twine,
Why do you, to her garland join
The meanest bud that falls from mine?
　Simplest of Swains! The World may see,
Whom CLOE loves! and who loves me!

CUPID MISTAKEN.

As, after noon, one summer's day,
　VENUS stood bathing in a river,
CUPID, a shooting, went that way;
　New strung his bow, new filled his quiver.

With skill, he chose his sharpest dart!
　With all his might, his bow he drew!
Aimed at his beauteous parent's heart;
　With certain speed the arrow flew!

'I faint! I die!' the Goddess cried,
　'O, cruel! couldst thou find none other
To wreck thy spleen on? Parricide!
　Like NERO, thou hast slain thy mother!'

Poor CUPID, sobbing, scarce could speak.
　'Indeed, Mamma, I did not know ye!
Alas! how easy my mistake!
　I took you for your likeness, CLOE!'

Matthew Prior.

The merchant, to secure his treasure,
   Conveys it in a borrowed name:
Euphelia serves to grace my measure;
   But Cloe is my real flame!

My softest verse, my darling lyre,
   Upon Euphelia's toilet lay;
When Cloe noted her desire
   That I should sing! that I should play!

My lyre I tune, my voice I raise;
   But with my Numbers mix my sighs!
And whilst I sing Euphelia's praise;
   I fix my soul on Cloe's eyes!

Fair Cloe blushed! Euphelia frowned!
   I sung and gazed! I played and trembled!
And Venus, to the Loves around
   Remarked, 'How ill we all dissembled!'

If Wine and Music have the power
   To ease the sickness of the soul,
Let Phœbus ev'ry string explore;
   And Bacchus fill the sprightly bowl!
Let them their friendly aid employ
   To make my Cloe's absence light!
And seek for pleasure, to destroy
   The sorrows of this life-long night!

But she to-morrow will return!
  VENUS! be thou to-morrow great!
Thy myrtles strow! thy odours burn!
  And meet thy fav'rite Nymph in State!
Kind Goddess! to no other Powers
  Let us to-morrow's blessings own!
Thy darling Loves shall guide the Hours;
  And all the day be thine alone!

IN IMITATION OF ANACREON.

  LET them censure! what care I?
The herd of Critics I defy!
Let the wretches know, I write
Regardless of their grace, or spite!
No! No! The Fair, the Gay, the Young,
Govern the Numbers of my Song!
All that they approve is sweet;
And all is sense that they repeat!

  Bid the warbling Nine retire!
VENUS! string thy Servant's lyre!
Love shall be my endless theme!
Pleasure shall triumph over Fame!
  And when these maxims I decline;
APOLLO! may thy fate be mine!
May I grasp at empty praise;
And lose the Nymph, to gain the Bays!

Matthew Prior.

THE LADY'S LOOKING-GLASS.

CELIA and I, the other day,
Walked o'er the sand-hills to the sea.
The setting sun adorned the coast;
His beams entire, his fierceness lost:
And, on the surface of the Deep,
The winds lay only not asleep.
  The Nymph did, like the scene appear,
Serenely joyous! calmly fair!
Soft fell her words, as flew the air!
With secret joy, I heard her say,
That she would never miss one day,
A walk so fine! a sight so gay!

  But, O, the change! The winds grow high!
Impending tempests charge the sky!
The lightning flies, the thunder roars;
And big waves lash the frightened shores!
  Struck with the horror of the sight,
She turns her head, and wings her flight;
And, trembling, vows she'll ne'er again
Approach the shore, or view the Main!

Matthew Prior.

'Once more, at least, look back!' said I,
'Thyself, in that large Glass descry!
When thou art in good humour drest,
When gentle Reason rules thy breast;
The sun, upon the calmest sea,
Appears not half so bright as thee!
'Tis then, that with delight I rove
Upon the boundless Depth of Love!
I bless my chain, I hand my oar;
Nor think on all I left on shore!

'But when vain doubts and groundless fear
Do that dear foolish bosom tear;
When the big lip, and wat'ry eye,
Tell me, the rising storm is nigh:
'Tis then, thou art yon angry Main,
Deformed by winds, and dashed by rain!
And the poor sailor that must try
Its fury, labours less than I!

'Shipwrecked, in vain to land I make!
While Love and Fate still drive me back.
Forced to dote on thee, thy own way;
I chide thee first, and then obey!
Wretched, when from thee; vexed, when nigh:
I, with thee, or without thee, die!

Matthew Prior.

THE FEMALE PHAETON.

Thus Kitty, beautiful and young,
   And wild as colt untamed,
Bespoke the Fair from whom she sprung;
   With little rage inflamed.

Inflamed with rage at sad restraint
   Which wise Mamma ordained;
And sorely vexed to play the Saint,
   While Wit and Beauty reigned.

'Shall I thumb holy books, confined
   With Abigails forsaken?
Kitty's for other things designed;
   Or I am much mistaken!

'Must Lady Jenny frisk about,
   And visit with her cousins?
At Balls, must she make all the rout;
   And bring home hearts by dozens?

'What has she better, pray, than I?
   What hidden charms to boast?
That all Mankind for her should die,
   Whilst I am scarce a Toast!

Matthew Prior.

'Dear Mamma! for once, let me,
 Unchained, my fortune try!
I'll have my Earl as well as she,
 Or know the reason why!

'I'll soon, with JENNY's pride quit score!
 Make all her Lovers fall!
They'll grieve, I was not loosed before!
 She, I was loosed at all!'

Fondness prevailed! Mamma gave way!
 KITTY, at heart's desire,
Obtained the chariot for the day;
 And set the World on fire!

READING ends in melancholy!
 Wine breeds vices and diseases!
Wealth 's but a care, and Love but folly;
 Only Friendship truly pleases!
My wealth, my books, my flask, my MOLLY,
 Farewell all, if Friendship ceases!

Matthew Prior.

CLOE HUNTING.

BEHIND her neck her comely tresses tied,
Her ivory quiver graceful by her side;
A hunting CLOE went! She lost her way;
And through the woods, uncertain, chanced to stray.
  APOLLO, passing by, beheld the Maid,
And, 'Sister dear, bright CYNTHIA! turn!' he said,
'The hunted hind lies close in yonder brake!'
  Loud CUPID laughed, to see the God's mistake;
And laughing, cried, 'Learn better, great Divine!
To know thy kindred; and to honour mine!
Rightly advised, far hence thy Sister seek,
Or on Meander's banks, or Latmus' peak!
But in this Nymph, my friend! *my* Sister know!
She draws my arrows, and she bends my bow!
Fair Thames, she haunts, and ev'ry neighb'ring grove
Sacred to soft recess and gentle love!
  'Go, with thy CYNTHIA! hurl the pointed spear
At the rough boar; or chase the flying deer!
I and my CLOE take a nobler aim!
At human hearts we fling; nor ever miss the game!'

THE GARLAND.

THE pride of ev'ry grove I chose,
  The Violet sweet, and Lily fair,
The dappled Pink, and blushing Rose,
  To deck my charming CLOE's hair.

Matthew Prior.

At Morn, the Nymph vouchsafed to place
    Upon her brow the various wreath;
The flowers less blooming than her face!
    The scent less fragrant than her breath!

The flowers she wore along the Day;
    And every Nymph and Shepherd said,
That, in her hair, they looked more gay
    Than glowing in their native bed!

Undressed at Evening, when she found
    Their odours lost, their colours past,
She changed her look; and on the ground,
    Her garland and her eye she cast.

That eye dropped sense distinct and clear,
    As any Muse's tongue could speak;
When from its lid, a pearly tear
    Ran trickling down her beauteous cheek.

Dissembling what I knew too well,
    'My Love! my life!' said I, 'explain
This change of humour! Prithee, tell!
    That falling tear—what does it mean?'

Matthew Prior.

She sighed! she smiled! and to the flowers
    Pointing, the lovely Moralist said,
'See, friend! in some few fleeting hours,
    See yonder, what a change is made!

'Ah! me! the blooming pride of May,
    And that of Beauty, are but one!
At Morn both flourish bright and gay;
    Both fade at Evening, pale, and gone!

'At Dawn, poor STELLA danced and sung;
    The am'rous Youth around her bowed!
At Night, her fatal knell was rung;
    I saw, and kissed, her in her shroud!

'Such as she is, who died To-day;
    Such I, alas! may be To-morrow!
Go, DAMON! bid thy Muse display
    The justice of thy CLOE's sorrow!'

THE CONVERSATION.
A TALE.

'IT always has been thought discreet
To know the company you meet;
And, sure, there may be secret danger
In talking much before a stranger!'

'Agreed! what then?'

       'Then, drink your ale!
I'll pledge you, and repeat my Tale!

'No matter where the scene is fixed,
The persons were but oddly mixed;
When sober DAMON thus began
(And DAMON is a clever man!):
'"I now grow old; but still, from youth,
Have held for Modesty and Truth!
The men who, by these sea-marks steer,
In Life's great voyage never err!
Upon this point, I dare defy
The World! I pause for a reply!"

Matthew Prior.

'" Sir! either is a good assistant!"
Said one who sat a little distant.
" Truth decks our speeches and our books;
And Modesty adorns our looks:
But farther progress we must take!
Not only born to Look and Speak;
The man must Act! The Stagyrite
Says thus, and says extremely right:
'"'Strict Justice is the sovereign guide,
That o'er our action should preside!
This Queen of Virtues is confest
To regulate and bind the rest!
Thrice happy, if you once can find
Her equal balance poise your mind!
All different graces soon will enter;
Like lines concurrent to their centre.'"

''Twas thus, in short, these two went on
With "Yea!" and "Nay!" and Pro and Con,
Through many points divinely dark,
And WATERLAND assaulting CLARK,
Till, in Theology half lost,
DAMON took up the *Evening Post*,
Confounded Spain, composed the North,
And deep in Politics held forth.

'" Methinks, we're in the like condition
As at the Treaty of Partition!

Matthew Prior.

That stroke (for all King WILLIAM's care!)
Begat another tedious war!
 ' "MATTHEW, who knew the whole intrigue,
Ne'er much approved that mystic League!
In the vile Utrecht Treaty too,
Poor man! he found enough to do!
Sometimes, to me he did apply;
But downright Dunstable was I!
And told him, where they were mistaken;
And counselled him to save his bacon!
 ' "But (pass his politics and prose!)
I never herded with his foes!
Nay! in his verses, as a friend,
I still found something to commend!
Sir! I excused his *Nut Brown Maid*;
Whate'er severer critics said!
Too far, I own, the Girl was tried!
The women, all were on my side!
For *Alma* I returned him thanks;
I liked her with her little pranks!
Indeed, poor *SOLOMON* in rhyme,
Was much too grave to be sublime!"

' PINDAR and DAMON scorn transition,
So on he ran a new division!
Till, out of breath, he turned to spit
(Chance often helps us more than Wit!).
 T'other that lucky moment took;
Just nicked the time, broke in, and spoke.

Matthew Prior.

'" Of all the gifts the Gods afford
(If we may take old TULLY's word!),
The greatest is a friend! whose love
Knows how to praise, and when reprove.
From such a treasure never part;
But hang the jewel on your heart!
'" And, pray, Sir! (it delights me!) tell,
You know this Author mighty well?"

'" Know him! D'ye question it? Ods-fish!
Sir! Does a beggar know his dish?
I loved him! As I told you, I
Advised him!" Here, a stander-by
Twitched DAMON gently by the cloak;
And thus unwilling silence broke:
'" DAMON! 'tis time we should retire!
The man you talk with is MAT. PRIOR!"'

Patron through life; and from thy birth, my friend!
DORSET! to thee, this Fable let me send!
With DAMON's lightness weigh thy solid worth;
The Foil is known to set the Diamond forth!
Let the feigned Tale this real Moral give!
How many DAMONS, how few DORSETS, live!

John Philips.

WHAT! put off with one denial!
And not make a second trial!
You might see my eyes consenting!
All about me was relenting!
Women, obliged to dwell in forms,
Forgive the Youth who boldly storms!

Lovers! when you sigh and languish,
When you tell us of your anguish;
To the Nymph, you'll be more pleasing,
When those sorrows you are ceasing!
We love to try, how far Men dare;
And never wish the foe should spare!

Anonymous.

THE SIGH.

By a Lady.

Gentlest air, the breath of Lovers!
   Vapour from a secret fire;
Which, by thee, itself discovers,
   Ere yet daring to aspire.

Softest note of whispered anguish!
   Harmony's most subtle part,
Striking, while thou seem'st to languish,
   Full upon the list'ner's heart!

Safest messenger of Passion!
   Stealing through a crowd of spies;
Which constrain the outward fashion,
   Close the lips, and guard the eyes.

Shapeless Sigh! None e'er can show thee!
   Framed but to assault the ear;
Yet, ere to their cost they know thee,
   Ev'ry Nymph may read thee—here!

Anonymous.

THE ROBBERY.

BELINDA! see, from yonder flowers
    The bee flies loaded to its cell!
Can you perceive what it devours?
    Are they impaired in show, or smell?

So, though I robbed you of a kiss
    Sweeter than their ambrosial dew;
Why are you angry at my bliss?
    Has it at all impoverished you?

'Tis by this cunning I contrive,
    In spite of your unkind reserve,
To keep my famished love alive;
    Which you inhumanly would starve.

William Harrison.

TO A VERY YOUNG LADY.

FLORELLA! when those eyes I see,
So innocently kind and free,
Ever fixed, and fixed on me!

Say, Why should I my time misspend,
With idle fears so long attend;
And lose the Lover in the Friend?

A year, or two, I could forbear;
But that some happier Youth, I fear,
May gain thy heart, and triumph there!

Then, dearest Girl! with me retire!
What Age should give, Love shall inspire!
And thou shalt ripen by my fire!

Anonymous.

LOVE IN FETTERS.

To PANTHEA.

LOVE, wearied with his roving flight,
Descending at th' approach of night,
Down to PANTHEA's bosom fled;
And made that Seat of Joy his bed.

Gently her heaving bosom rose,
And seemed to court him to repose;
Nestling, he folds his wings, to creep
Between her breasts for sweeter sleep.

Pleased and transported with the joy,
She laughed at the deluded Boy;
And did a stratagem prepare
To keep the wanton pris'ner there.

She took a various coloured braid,
Of purple, gold, and scarlet made;
'Now, Youngster!' said the cruel Fair,
'You shall PANTHEA's fetters wear!'

But when surprised, he waking found
His shackled limbs, and pinions bound,
Sighing, he wept; and begged, She'd please
To give her captive a release!

'Sly Youth,' says she, 'would you so soon
Quit your apartments, and be gone!
No, my dear Rover! first discharge
Your quarters, ere you're set at large!'

'Then, for a bribe,' said he, 'to go,
My quiver take, and take my bow!
Nor can I greater triumphs boast,
Than that my Arms to you were lost!'

And now those shafts are his no more;
His bow and ensigns of his power!
PANTHEA now commands LOVE's darts!
All eyes she charms; and wounds all hearts!

A DIALOGUE
BETWEEN SURLY AND BEAU.

SURLY. Prithee, tell me, What a Beau is?
   Thou who art so famed for one!

BEAU. He's a person of great prowess!
   By these marks he may be known.

   Though his eyebrows black as jet are,
   Yet his wig is white as snow!
   Ev'ry hour he writes some letter,
   Or receives some *billet-doux!*

Anonymous.

Well, or ill, he briskly dances;
   And his arms are never still!
Casting about am'rous glances,
   Such as seldom fail to kill.

Sits all day among the Ladies;
   Sees them paint, and sees them patch:
In their eyes still looking babies,
   Some rich heir in hope to catch.

Some French tune he 's ever humming;
   Though he cannot sing one note!
Or, with Air and grace becoming,
   Gives ill-scented snuff about!

Under his left arm a bamboo,
   Ribbon dangling at his sword;
Tells you, all he has, or can do;
   And whom last he laid on board. . . .

SURLY. If this be your accomplished Beau;
   He is the oddest fool I know!

John Byrom, F.R.S.

My time, O, ye Muses! was happily spent,
When PHEBE went with me wherever I went,
Ten thousand sweet pleasures I felt in my breast,
Sure, never fond Shepherd like COLIN was blest!
But now she is gone, and has left me behind;
What a marvellous change on a sudden I find!
When things were as fine as could possibly be,
I thought 'twas the Spring; but, alas! it was she!

With such a companion, to tend a few sheep,
To rise up and play, or to lie down and sleep;
I was so good-humoured, so cheerful and gay,
My heart was as light as a feather all day!
But now I so cross and so peevish am grown,
So strangely uneasy, as never was known!
My Fair One is gone, and my joys are all drowned,
And my heart—I am sure, it weighs more than a pound!

John Byrom, F.R.S.

The fountain, that wont to run sweetly along
And dance to soft murmurs the pebbles among,
Thou know'st, little CUPID! if PHEBE were there,
'Twas Pleasure to look at! 'twas Music to hear!
But now she is absent, I walk by its side,
And still, as it murmurs, do nothing but chide!
'Must you be so cheerful, while I go in pain?
Peace there, with your bubbling; and hear me complain!'

My lambkins, around me would oftentimes play.
And PHEBE and I were as joyful as they;
How pleasant their sporting, how happy their time,
When Spring, Love, and Beauty were all in their prime!
But now, in their frolics, when by me they pass;
I fling at their fleeces a handful of grass!
'Be still then!' I cry, 'for it makes me quite mad,
To see you so merry, while I am so sad!'

My dog I was ever well pleasèd to see
Come wagging his tail to my Fair One and me;
And PHEBE was pleased too, and to my dog said,
'Come hither, poor fellow!' and patted his head.
But now, when he's fawning, I, with a sour look,
Cry, 'Sirrah!' and give him a blow with my crook:
And I'll give him another! For why should not Tray
Be as dull as his master, when PHEBE's away?

When walking with PHEBE, what sights have I seen!
How fair was the flower! how fresh was the green!
What a lovely appearance the trees and the shade,
The cornfields and hedges, and every thing, made!
  But now she has left me, though all are still there,
They none of them now so delightful appear!
'Twas naught but the magic, I find, of her eyes
Made so many beautiful prospects arise!

  Sweet music went with us both, all the wood through,
The lark, linnet, throstle, and nightingale too.
Winds over us whispered. Flocks by us did bleat;
And chirp went the grasshopper under our feet.
  But now she is absent, though still they sing on,
The woods are but lonely! the melody's gone!
Her voice, in the consort, as now I have found,
Gave ev'ry thing else its agreeable sound.

  Rose! what is become of thy delicate hue?
And where is the Violet's beautiful blue?
Does aught of its sweetness the blossom beguile?
That meadow, those Daisies, why do they not smile?
  Ah! rivals! I see what it was, that you drest
And made yourselves fine for! A place in her breast!
You put on your colours, to pleasure her eye;
To be plucked by her hand, on her bosom to die!

John Byrom, F.R.S.

How slowly Time creeps, till my PHEBE return!
While amidst the soft Zephyr's cold breezes I burn.
Methinks, if I knew whereabouts he would tread;
I could breathe on his wings! and 'twould melt down
    the lead.
Fly swifter, ye minutes! bring hither my Dear!
And rest so much longer for 't, when she is here.
'Ah! COLIN! old Time is full of delay;
Nor will budge one foot faster, for all thou canst say!'

Will no pitying Power, that hears me complain,
Or cure my disquiet, or soften my pain?
'To be cured, thou must, COLIN! thy Passion remove;
But what Swain is so silly to live without love?'
No, Deity! bid the dear Nymph to return!
For ne'er was poor Shepherd so sadly forlorn.
Ah! what shall I do? I shall die with despair!
Take heed, all ye Swains! how ye part with your Fair!

GOD bless the King! I mean the Faith's Defender!
GOD bless (No harm in blessing!) the Pretender!
But who Pretender is, or who is King—
GOD bless us all!—that 's quite another thing!

Ambrose Philips.

A HYMN TO VENUS.

'O, VENUS! Beauty of the skies!
To whom a thousand Temples rise,
Gaily false in gentle smiles,
Full of love-perplexing wiles;
O, Goddess! from my heart remove
The wasting cares and pangs of love!

'If ever thou hast kindly heard
A Song in soft distress preferred;
Propitious to my tuneful vow,
O, gentle Goddess! hear me now!
Descend, thou bright, immortal guest,
In all thy radiant charms confessed!

'Thou, once, didst leave almighty JOVE;
And all the golden roofs above!
The car thy wanton sparrows drew,
Hovering in air, they lightly flew;
As to my bower they winged their way,
I saw their quiv'ring pinions play!

'The birds dismissed, while you remain,
Bore back their empty car again.
Then you, with looks divinely mild,
In ev'ry heavenly feature smiled,
And asked, What new complaints I made?
And, Why I called you to my aid?

Ambrose Philips.

'What frenzy in my bosom raged?
And by what care to be assuaged?
What gentle Youth I would allure,
Whom in my artful toils secure?
"Who does thy tender heart subdue?
Tell me, my SAPPHO! tell me, Who?

'"Though now he shuns thy longing arms;
He soon shall court thy slighted charms!
Though now thy off'rings he despise;
He soon to thee shall sacrifice!
Though now he freeze; he soon shall burn,
And be thy victim in his turn!"

'Celestial Visitant! once more,
Thy needful presence I implore!
In pity, come, and ease my griefs!
Bring my distempered soul relief!
Favour thy Suppliant's hidden fires;
And give me all my heart desires!'

BLESSED as th' immortal Gods is he,
The Youth who fondly sits by thee;
And hears and sees thee, all the while,
Softly speak and sweetly smile!

Ambrose Philips.

'Twas this deprived my soul of rest,
And raised such tumults in my breast;
For, while I gazed, in transport tossed,
My breath was gone! my voice was lost!

My bosom glowed! The subtle flame
Ran quickly through all my vital frame!
O'er my dim eyes a darkness hung!
My ears, with hollow murmurs rung!

In dewy damps, my limbs were chilled!
My blood with gentle horrors thrilled!
My feeble pulse forgot to play;
I fainted, sunk, and died away!

   WHY we love, and why we hate,
      Is not granted us to know!
   Random Chance, or wilful Fate,
      Guides the shaft from CUPID's bow!

   If on me ZELINDA frown;
      Madness 'tis in me to grieve!
   Since her will is not her own,
      Why should I uneasy live?

   If I for ZELINDA die,
      Deaf to poor MIZELLA's cries;
   Ask me not the reason Why?
      Seek the riddle in the skies!

Ambrose Philips.

THE STRAY NYMPH.

CEASE your music, gentle Swains!
Saw ye DELIA cross the plains?
Every thicket, every grove,
Have I ranged, to find my Love!
A kid, a lamb, my flock, I give!
Tell me only, Doth she live?

White her skin as mountain snow!
In her cheek the roses blow;
And her eye is brighter far
Than the beamy Morning Star!
When her ruddy lip ye view,
'Tis a berry moist with dew!
And her breath—O, 'tis a gale
Passing o'er a fragrant vale!
Passing when a friendly shower
Freshens every herb and flower!
Wide her bosom opens, gay
As the primrose dell in May!
Sweet as violet borders growing
Over fountains ever flowing!
Like the tendrils of the vine
Do her auburn tresses twine!
Glossy ringlets all behind,
Streaming buxom to the wind;
When along the lawn she bounds,
Light as hind before the hounds!

And the youthful ring she fires,
Hopeless in their fond desires,
As her flitting feet advance,
Wanton in the winding dance.

Tell me, Shepherds! have ye seen
My delight, my Love, my Queen?

From WHITE's and WILL's,
 To purling rills,
The love-sick STREPHON flies!
 There, full of woe,
 His Numbers flow;
And all in rhyme he dies!

 The fair Coquette,
 With feigned regret,
Invites him back to Town;
 But when, in tears,
 The Youth appears;
She meets him with a frown!

 Full oft the Maid,
 This prank had played,
'Till angry STREPHON swore;
 And what is strange,
 Though loth to change,
Would never see her more!

ALEXANDER POPE.

TO LADY WINCHILSEA.

OCCASIONED BY FOUR VERSES IN
'THE RAPE OF THE LOCK.'

IN vain you boast poetic names of yore;
And cite those SAPPHOS we admire no more!
Fate doomed the fall of every Female Wit;
But doomed it then, when first ARDELIA writ!
  Of all examples, by the World confest,
I knew ARDELIA could not quote the best!
Who, like her Mistress on BRITANNIA's throne,
Fights, and subdues, in quarrels not her own.
  To write their praise, you but, in vain, essay!
Even while you write, you take that praise away!
Light to the stars, the sun does thus restore;
And shines himself, till they are seen no more!

LADY WINCHILSEA.

ANSWER TO THE FOREGOING VERSES.

    DISARMED with so genteel an Air,
      The contest I give o'er!
    Yet, ALEXANDER! have a care,
      And shock the Sex no more!

We rule the World, our life's whole race!
　　Men but assume that right:
First, slaves to ev'ry tempting face;
　　Then, martyrs to our spite!

You, of one ORPHEUS, sure, have read!
　　Who would like you have writ,
Had he in London town been bred,
　　And polished too his wit.

But he, poor soul! thought all was well,
　　And great should be his fame!
When he had left his Wife in Hell;
　　And birds and beasts could tame.

Yet vent'ring then, with scoffing rhymes,
　　The women to incense;
Resenting heroines of those Times
　　Soon punished his offence!

And as the Hebrus rolled his skull
　　And harp besmeared with blood;
They, clashing as the waves grew full,
　　Still harmonized the flood.

But you, our follies gently treat,
　　And spin so fine the thread;
You need not fear his awkward fate!
　　The *Lock* won't cost the head!

Our admiration you command,
    For all that 's gone before;
What next we look for at your hand,
    Can only raise it more!

Yet soothe the Ladies, I advise!
    (As me too, pride has wrought!)
We're born to wit; but to be wise,
    By admonitions taught.

PERSUADE me not, there is a grace
    Proceeds from SILVIA's voice, or lute,
Against MIRANDA's charming face,
    To make her hold the least dispute!

Music, which tunes the Soul for Love,
    And stirs up all our soft desires,
Does but the growing flame improve,
    Which powerful Beauty first inspires.

Thus, whilst with art she plays and sings,
    I, to MIRANDA, standing by,
Impute the music of the strings;
    And all the melting words apply!

A NOCTURNAL REVERIE.

In such a night, when every louder wind
Is to its distant cavern safe confined,
And only gentle ZEPHYR fans his wings;
And lonely PHILOMEL, still waking, sings,
Or from some tree famed for the owl's delight,
She, hollowing clear, directs the wand'rer right;
In such a night, when passing clouds give place,
Or thinly veil the heavens' mysterious face;
When, in some river, overhung with green,
The waving moon and trembling leaves are seen;
When freshened grass now bears itself upright,
And makes cool banks to pleasing rest invite;
Whence spring the woodbine and the bramble-rose,
And where the sleepy cowslip sheltered grows;
While now a paler hue the foxglove takes,
Yet checkers still with red the dusky brakes;
  When scattered glowworms, but in twilight fine,
Shew trivial beauties, watch their hour to shine;
Whilst Salisb'ry stands the test of every light
In perfect charms, and perfect virtue bright;
  When odours, which declined repelling day,
Through temp'rate air uninterrupted stray;

Anne Finch, Countess of Winchilsea, &c.

When darkened groves their softest shadows wear,
And falling waters we distinctly hear;
When through the gloom more venerable shows
Some ancient fabric, awful in repose;
While sunburnt hills their swarthy looks conceal,
And swelling haycocks thicken up the vale;
  When the loosed horse now, as his pasture leads,
Comes slowly grazing through th' adjoining meads;
Whose stealing pace and lengthened shade we fear,
Till torn-up forage in his teeth we hear;
When nibbling sheep at large pursue their food,
And unmolested kine re-chew the cud;
When curlews cry beneath the village walls,
And to her straggling brood the partridge calls;
Their short-lived Jubilee the creatures keep,
Which but endures whilst tyrant Man does sleep;
  When a sedate content the spirit feels,
And no fierce light disturbs, whilst it reveals;
But silent musings urge the mind to seek
Something too high for syllables to speak;
Till the free Soul, to a compos'dness charmed,
Finding the elements of rage disarmed,
O'er all below a solemn quiet grown,
Joys in th' inferior world, and thinks it like her own:
  In such a night, let me abroad remain,
Till morning breaks, and all 's confused again!
Our cares, our toils, our clamours, are renewed;
Or pleasures, seldom reached, again pursued.

Archdeacon Thomas Parnell, D.D.

My days have been so wondrous free!
  The little birds, that fly
With careless ease from tree to tree,
  Were but as blessed as I!

Ask gliding waters, If a tear
  Of mine increased their stream?
Or ask the flying gales, If e'er
  I lent a sigh to them?

But now my former days retire,
  And I'm by Beauty caught!
The tender chains of sweet desire
  Are fixed upon my thought!

An eager hope within my breast
  Does ev'ry doubt control;
And charming NANCY stands confest
  The fav'rite of my soul!

Ye nightingales, ye twisting pines,
  Ye Swains that haunt the grove,
Ye gentle echoes, breezy winds,
  Ye close retreats of Love,

With all of Nature, all of Art,
  Assist the dear design!
O, teach a young unpractised heart
  To make her ever mine!

Archdeacon Thomas Parnell, D.D.

The very thought of Change I hate,
  As much as of Despair;
And hardly covet to be Great,
  Unless it be for her!

'Tis true, the Passion, in my mind,
  Is mixed with soft distress;
Yet while the Fair I love is kind,
  I cannot wish it less!

'WHEN thy beauty appears,
  In its graces and Airs,
As bright as an Angel new dropped from the sky;
At distance I gaze, and am awed by my fears;
  So strangely you dazzle my eye!

'But when, without art,
  Your kind thoughts you impart;
When your love runs in blushes through every vein;
When it darts from your eyes, when it pants in your
    heart;
  Then I know you're a Woman again!'

'There's a Passion and pride
  In our Sex,' She replied,
And thus (might I gratify both!) I would do!
Still an Angel appear to each Lover beside;
  But still be a Woman to you!'

ANACREONTIC.

Gay Bacchus, liking Estcourt's wine,
    A noble meal bespoke us;
And for the guests, that were to dine,
    Brought Comus, Love, and Jocus.

The God, near Cupid drew his chair;
    Near Comus, Jocus placed:
Thus Wine makes Love forget its care;
    And Mirth exalts a feast.

The more to please the spritely God!
    Each sweet engaging Grace
Put on some clothes, to come abroad;
    And took a Waiter's place.

Then Cupid named, at every Glass,
    A Lady of the sky;
While Bacchus swore, he'd drink the Lass!
    And had it bumper-high.

Fat Comus tossed his brimmers o'er,
    And always got the most;
Jocus took care to fill him more;
    Whene'er he missed the Toast.

Archdeacon Thomas Parnell, D.D.

Then called, and drank at every touch;
    He filled, and drank again!
And if the Gods can take too much,
    'Tis said, they did so then!

[Free jests run all the table round,
    And with the wine conspire
(While they, by sly reflection wound)
    To set their heads on fire.]

Gay BACCHUS, little CUPID stung,
    By reck'ning his deceits;
And CUPID mocked his stammering tongue,
    With all his stagg'ring gaits.

And JOCUS drolled on COMUS' ways,
    And tales without a jest;
While COMUS called his witty Plays
    But waggeries at best.

Such talk soon set them all at odds;
    And, had I HOMER's pen,
I'd sing ye, How they drunk, like Gods;
    And how they fought, like men.

To part the fray, the Graces fly;
    Who make them soon agree!
Nay, had the Furies' selves been nigh,
    They still were three to three!

Archdeacon Thomas Parnell, D.D.

BACCHUS appeased, raised CUPID up;
  And gave him back his bow;
But kept some darts to stir the cup
  Where Sack and sugar flow.

JOCUS took COMUS' rosy crown,
  And gaily wore the prize:
And thrice, in mirth, he pushed him down,
  As thrice he strove to rise.

Then CUPID sought the myrtle grove,
  Where VENUS did recline;
And, VENUS close embracing LOVE,
  They joined to rail at Wine.

And COMUS, loudly cursing Wit,
  Rolled off to some retreat,
Where boon companions gravely sit
  In fat unwieldy State.

BACCHUS and JOCUS still behind,
  For one fresh Glass prepare!
They kiss, and are exceeding kind;
  And vow to be sincere.

But part in time (whoever hear
  This our instructive Song!);
For though such friendships may be dear,
  They can't continue long!

Archdeacon Thomas Parnell, D.D.

THYRSIS, a young and am'rous Swain,
Saw two, the Beauties of the plain;
   Who both his heart subdue.
Gay CŒLIA's eyes were dazzling fair;
SABINA's easy shape and Air,
   With softer magic drew.

He haunts the stream, he haunts the grove,
Lives in a fond Romance of Love;
   And seems for each to die!
Till each, a little spiteful grown,
SABINA, CŒLIA's shape ran down;
   And she, SABINA's eye.

Their envy made the Shepherd find
Those eyes which Love could only blind;
   So set the Lover free!
No more he haunts the grove, or stream;
Or with a True-Love Knot and name,
   Engraves a wounded tree!

'Ah, CŒLIA!' sly SABINA cried,
'Though neither love; we're both denied!
Now, to support the Sex's pride,
   Let either fix the dart!'
'Poor Girl!' says CŒLIA, 'say no more!'
For should the Swain but one adore,
That spite, which broke his chains before,
   Would break the other's heart!'

Archdeacon Thomas Parnell, D.D.

LOVE IN DISGUISE.

To stifle Passion is no easy thing!
A heart in love is always on the wing!
    The bold betrayer flutters still,
    And fans the breath prepared to tell:
    It melts the tongue, and tunes the throat,
    And moves the lips to form the note;
      And when the speech is lost,
      It then sends out its ghost,
        A little sigh,
        To say, 'We die!'
'Tis strange, the air, that cools, a flame should prove!
But wonder not! It is the air of love!

Yet, CHLORIS! I can make my love look well;
And cover bleeding wounds I can't conceal!
    My words such art-ful accents break,
    You think I rather act than speak!
    My sighs, enlivened through a smile,
    Your unsuspecting thoughts beguile!
      My eyes are varied so,
      You can't their wishes know!
        And I'm so gay,
        You think I play!
Happy contrivance! such as can't be prized!
To live in love; and yet to live disguised!

Anonymous.

LOVE'S RELIEF.

A WRETCH, long tortured with disdain,
That hourly pined, but pined in vain;
At length, the God of Wine addrest,
The refuge of a wounded breast.

'Vouchsafe, O, Power! thy healing aid!
Teach me to gain the cruel Maid!
Thy juices take the Lover's part,
Flush his wan looks, and cheer his heart!'

Thus to the jolly God he cried;
And thus the jolly God replied.
'Give whining o'er! Be brisk and gay;
And quaff this sneaking Form away!'

'With dauntless mien approach the Fair!
The way to conquer is to dare!'
The Swain pursued the God's advice;
The Nymph was now no longer nice.

She smiled, and spoke the Sex's mind,
'When you grow daring; we grow kind!
Men to themselves are most severe;
And make us tyrants by their fear!'

Anonymous.

A SILLY Shepherd wooed; but wist not
　How he might his Mistress' favour gain.
On a time, they met; but kissed not!
　Ever after that, he sued in vain!
　　Blame her not, alas! though She said 'Nay!'
　　To him that might; but fled away!

Time perpetually is changing,
　Every moment alteration brings,
Love and Beauty still estranging.
　Women are, alas! but wanton things!
　　He that will his Mistress' favour gain,
　　Must take her in a merry vein!

A woman's fancy 's like a fever;
　Or an ague, that doth come by fits!
Hot and cold, but constant never;
　Even as the pleasant humour hits.
　　Sick, and well again; and well and sick;
　　In love it is a woman's trick!

Anonymous.

Now she will; and then she will not!
  Put her to the trial, if once she smile!
Silly Youth! thy fortunes spill not!
  Ling'ring labours oft themselves beguile!
    He that knocks, and can't get in;
    His pick-lock is not worth a pin!

A woman's 'Nay!' is no denial!
  Silly Youths of love are served so!
Put her to a further trial!
  Haply, she'll take it, and say 'No!'
    For it is a trick which women use;
    What they love, they will refuse!

Silly Youth! why dost thou dally,
  Having got time and season fit?
Then, never stand, 'Sweet! shall I? shall I?'
  Nor too much commend an after-wit!
    For he that will not, when he may;
    When he will, he shall have 'Nay!'

Nicholas Rowe, P.L.

THE RECONCILEMENT BETWEEN JACOB TONSON AND MR. CONGREVE.

IN IMITATION OF HORACE, BOOK III, ODE IX.

TONSON. WHILE at my house in Fleet street once you lay,
How merrily, dear Sir! time passed away!
While I partook your wine, your wit, and mirth;
I was the happiest creature on 'God's yearth'![1]

CONGREVE. While, in your early days of reputation,
You for Blue Garters had not such a Passion;
While yet you did not use, as now your trade is,
To drink with noble Lords, and toast their Ladies:
Thou, JACOB TONSON! wert, to my conceiving,
The cheerfullest, best, honest fellow living!

TONSON. I'm in with Captain VANBRUGH at the present,
A most sweet-natured Gentleman, and pleasant!
He writes your Comedies, draws Schemes and
   Models;
And builds Dukes' houses upon very odd hills!
For him, so much I dote on him, that I
(If I were sure to go to heaven!) would die!

[1] TONSON senior, his dialect.

Nicholas Rowe, P.L.

CONGREVE. TEMPLE and DELAVALL are now my party,
Men that are *tam MERCURIO*, both *quam MARTE*.
And though for them, I shall scarce go to Heaven;
Yet I can drink with them, six nights in seven!

TONSON. What if from VAN's dear arms I should retire;
And once more warm my 'bunnians'[1] at your fire!
If I to Bow street should invite you home,
And set a bed up in my dining-room;
Tell me, dear Mr. CONGREVE! would you come?

CONGREVE. Though the gay Sailor and the gentle Knight
Were ten times more my joy and heart's delight;
Though civil persons they; you ruder were,
And had more humours than a dancing bear:
Yet, for your sake, I'd bid them both 'Adieu!'
And live and die, dear COB! with only you!

COLIN'S COMPLAINT.

DESPAIRING, beside a clear stream,
   A Shepherd forsaken was laid;
And while a false Nymph was his theme,
   A willow supported his head.
The wind, that blew over the plain,
   To his sighs, with a sigh did reply;
And the brook, in return to his pain,
   Ran mournfully murmuring by.

---

[1] JACOB's term for his corns.

Nicholas Rowe, P.L.

'Alas! silly Swain that I was!'
   Thus, sadly complaining, he cried,
'When first I beheld that fair face,
   'Twere better, by far, I had died!
She talked; and I blessed the dear tongue!
   When She smiled, 'twas a pleasure too great!
I listened, and cried, when She sung,
   "Was nightingale ever so sweet?"

'How foolish I was to believe
   She could dote on so lowly a Clown!
Or that her fond heart would not grieve
   To forsake the fine folk of the Town!
To think that a Beauty so gay,
   So kind and so constant would prove;
Or go clad like our Maidens, in grey;
   Or live in a cottage on love!

'What though I have skill to complain,
   Though the Muses my temples have crowned;
What though, when they hear my soft strain,
   The Virgins sit weeping around;
Ah! COLIN! thy hopes are in vain!
   Thy pipe and thy laurel resign!
Thy False One inclines to a Swain,
   Whose music is sweeter than thine!

Nicholas Rowe, P.L.

'And you, my companions so dear!
   Who sorrow to see me betrayed,
Whatever I suffer; forbear,
   Forbear to accuse the false Maid!
Though through the wide world I should range;
   'Tis in vain from my fortune to fly!
'Twas hers to be false and to change;
   'Tis mine to be constant and die!

'If, while my hard fate I sustain,
   In her breast any pity is found;
Let her come, with the Nymphs of the plain,
   And see me laid low in the ground!
The last humble boon that I crave,
   Is to shade me with cypress and yew;
And when she looks down on my grave,
   Let her own, that her Shepherd was true!

'Then, to her New Love let her go,
   And deck her in golden array!
Be finest at ev'ry fine Show,
   And frolic it all the long day!
While COLIN, forgotten and gone,
   No more shall be talked of, or seen;
Unless when, beneath the pale moon,
   His ghost shall glide over the Green.'

Aaron Hill.

O, FORBEAR to bid me slight her!
  Soul and Senses take her part!
Could my death itself delight her;
  Life should leap, to leave my heart!
    Strong, though soft, a Lover's chain!
    Charmed with woe; and pleased with pain!

Though the tender flame were dying,
  Love would light it at her eyes!
Or her tuneful voice applying,
  Through my ear, my soul surprise!
    Deaf, I see the fate I shun!
    Blind, I hear I am undone!

'GENTLE LOVE! this hour befriend me!
  To my eyes resign thy dart!
Notes of melting music lend me,
  To dissolve a frozen heart!

'Chill as mountain snow her bosom;
  Though I tender language use!
'Tis, by cold indifference, frozen
  To my arms, and to my Muse!

'See! my dying eyes are pleading,
  Where a breaking heart appears!
For thy pity interceding,
  With the eloquence of tears!

'While the lamp of life is fading;
  And beneath thy coldness dies!
Death, my ebbing pulse invading,
  Take my soul into thy eyes!'

THE LETTER.

I took the paper in my trembling hand;
  Which, having writ your name, my pen confined,
And forced my hasty will to make a stand,
  While love's imperious tempest shook my mind.

Cold languid sweats fall gently from my brow;
  And while I strive to write 'I love you well!'
My conscious heart whispers, 'Thou know'st not how!
  Alas! thou lov'st him more than thou canst tell!'

What then remains, in this extreme, to do?
  Say, trembling hand! Cold icy heart, declare!
'You guide my fate! I'm blessed, if you prove true!
  And nothing, sure, is false, that looks so fair!

'Some Maids are ruined, and no pity find;
  But their deceivers were not made like mine!
Ah! who can see thy face, and not be kind?
  Or stand the charms of such a tongue as thine?'

Anonymous.

FAREWELL, my Mistress! I'll be gone!
I have friends to wait upon!
Think you, I'll myself confine
To your humours, Lady mine!
No! Your louring looks do say,
''Twill be a rainy drinking day;
To the Tavern let 's away!'

There have I a Mistress got
Cloistered in a Pottle Pot!
Plump and bounding, soft and fair,
Buxom, sweet, and debonair;
And they call her, 'Sack,' my Dear! . . .

Yet, if thou wilt take the pain
To be kind yet once again!
And with thy smiles but call me back;
Thou shalt be the Lady Sack!
O, then try! and you shall see
What a loving soul I'll be,
When I'm drunk with none but thee!

John Sheffield, Duke of Buckingham.

THE RECONCILEMENT.

Come, let us now resolve at last,
    To live and love in quiet;
We'll tie the knot so very fast,
    That Time shall ne'er untie it!

The truest joys they seldom prove,
    Who free from quarrels live.
'Tis the most tender part of love,
    Each other to forgive!

When least I seemed concerned, I took
    No pleasure, nor no rest!
And when I feigned an angry look,
    Alas! I loved you best!

Own but the same to me; you'll find
    How blessed will be our fate!
O, to be happy! to be kind!
    Sure, never is too late.

John Sheffield, Duke of Buckingham.

THE ELECTION OF A POET LAUREATE
IN 1719.

A FAMOUS Assembly was summoned of late.
To crown a new Laureate, came PHŒBUS in State;
With all that MONTFAUCON himself could desire,
His bow, laurel, harp, and abundance of fire.

At Bartlemew Fair ne'er did Bullies so justle;
No County Election e'er made such a bustle!
From garret, Mint, tavern, they all post away;
Some thirsting for Sack; some ambitious for Bay!

All came with full confidence, flushed with vain hope,
From CIBBER and D'URFEY, to PRIOR and POPE.
PHŒBUS smiled on these last; but yet ne'ertheless
Said, He hoped they had got enough by the Press!

With a huge mountain-load of heroical lumber,
Which from TONSON to CURLL ev'ry press had groaned under,
Came BLACKMORE, and cried, 'Look! all these are my Lays!
But, at present, I beg you'd but read my *Essays!*'

John Sheffield, Duke of Buckingham.

Lampooners and Critics rushed in like a tide.
Stern DENNIS and GILDON came first side by side.
APOLLO confessed, That their lashes had stings;
But Beadles and Hangmen were never chose Kings!

STEELE long had so cunningly managed the Town;
He could not be blamed for expecting the crown!
APOLLO demurred as to granting his wish;
But wished him good luck to his Project of Fish!

Lame CONGREVE, unable such things to endure,
Of APOLLO begged either a crown, or a cure!
To refuse such a Writer, APOLLO was loth,
And almost inclined to have granted him both.

When BUCKINGHAM came, he scarce cared to be seen,
Till PHŒBUS desired his old friend to walk in.
But a Laureate Peer had never been known!
The Commoners claimed that Place as their own!

Yet if the kind God had been ne'er so inclined
To break an old rule; yet he well knew his mind:
Who of such preferment would only make sport,
And laughed at all suitors for Places at Court!

Notwithstanding this law, yet LANSDOWNE was named;
But APOLLO, with kindness, his indolence blamed!
And said, He would choose him; but that he should fear
An employment of trouble he never could bear!

John Sheffield, Duke of Buckingham.

A Prelate for wit and for eloquence famed
APOLLO soon missed; and he needs not be named!
Since (amidst a whole Bench, of which some are so bright)
No one of them shines so learned and polite!

To SHIPPEN, APOLLO was cold with respect;
Since he, for the State could the Muses neglect:
But said, In a greater Assembly he shined,
And Places were things he had ever declined!

TR—P, Y—G, and VANBRUGH expected reward
For some things writ well: but APOLLO declared,
That one was too flat, the other too rough;
And the third, sure, already had Places enough!

Pert BUDGELL came next, and demanding the Bays,
Said, 'Those Works must be good, which had ADDI-
    SON's praise!'
But APOLLO replied, 'Child EUSTACE! 'tis known
Most Authors will praise whatsoever 's their own!'

Then PHILIPS came forth, as starch as a Quaker,
Whose simple profession 's a *Pastoral*-maker.
APOLLO advised him, From Playhouse to keep;
And pipe to nought else but his dog and his sheep!

HUGHES, FENTON, and GAY came last in the Train;
Too modest to ask for the Crown they would gain.
PHŒBUS thought them too bashful, and said, 'They
    would need
More boldness, if ever they hoped to succeed!'

John Sheffield, Duke of Buckingham.

APOLLO, now driv'n to a cursèd quandary,
Was wishing for SWIFT, or the famed Lady MARY.
Nay! had honest TOM SOUTHERNE but been within call—
But, at last, he grew wanton; and laughed at them all!

And so, 'spying one who came only to gaze,
A hater of Verse and despiser of Plays,
To him, in great form, without any delay,
(Though a zealous Fanatic!) presented the Bay.

All the Wits stood astonished, at hearing the God
So gravely pronounce an election so odd;
And though PRIOR and POPE only laughed in his face,
Most others were ready to sink in the place.

Yet some thought the vacancy open was kept,
Concluding the bigot would never accept:
But the hypocrite told them, 'He well understood,
Though the function was wicked, the stipend was good!'

At last, in rushed EUSDEN, and cried, 'Who shall have it
But I, the true Laureate! to whom the King gave it!'
APOLLO begged pardon, and granted his claim;
But vowed though, till then, he ne'er heard of his name!

Rev. Laurence Eusden, P.L.

TO MR. ——.

You ask, my friend! How I can Delia prize;
When Myra's shape I view, or Cynthia's eyes?
No tedious answer shall create you pain;
For beauty, if but beauty, I disdain!
'Tis not a mien, that can my will control;
A speaking body with a silent soul!
The loveliest face to me not lovely shows,
From the sweet lips if melting nonsense flows!
Nor must the tuneful Chloris be my choice!
An earthly mind ill suits a heavenly voice!

What though my Delia not decayed appears,
'She wants,' you cry, 'the gaudy bloom of years!'
True! But good sense perpetual joys will bring!
Her wit is ever youthful as the Spring! . . .

Not so my Delia shall consume her charms;
But rise, each morn, more beauteous from my arms!
With envious swiftness, rolling years may move,
Impair her glories; not impair my love!
Time's wasteful rage, the Husband shall despise;
And view the Wife still with the Bridegroom's eyes! . . .

Hon. Mary Monk.

A TALE.

A BAND of CUPIDS, th' other day,
Together met to laugh and play.
When, on a sudden, 'Come, who flies?'
Says one. 'But whither?' t' other cries.
'Why, whither, but to CLOE's eyes!'
Replied a third. The wanton crew
(Like swarms of bees to roses) flew
Around the beauteous CLOE's face,
And crowded hard to get a place.
  This on her nether lip does fix;
Whilst on her cheek another sticks.
This swings upon her flowing hair.
In her fair eyes, a lovely pair
Of Youths stand, with their torches lit.
Two others on her eyebrows sit,
Each with his bow. Amongst the rest,
One missed her chin; and on her breast
Fell headlong: but soon, looking up, did cry,
'None of you've got so good a place as I!'

Leonard Welsted.

THE PICTURE OF A FINE APRIL MORNING.

' THE snows are melted, and the frosts are past;
Nor do we longer dread the wintry blast!
What garland shall AMINTOR now design?
What wreath, ZELINDA! round thy temples twine?
 ' The dawning year revives the Poet's fire;
Soft strains of love returning suns inspire!
In every wood, behold, in every glade,
Th' unsullied verdure, and the growing shade!
All Nature, like a Bride, emerges bright;
And her lap teems, luxuriant with delight.
 ' O'er tepid plains the tempering zephyrs pass,
Call forth the bursting leaves, and spring the grass!
Afresh the painted pansy rears its head.
The whitened meadow starry daisies spread.
The birds sweet warble from the sappy boughs;
And Swains in tuneful sighs renew their vows.
 ' Inspire, O, blooming Maid! my artless Lay;
While I recall our first auspicious day.
The dawn, my Fair! when early I addressed
My tender suit; and sighed upon thy breast!

 ' ZELINDA blushed; a blush the morning wore!
ZELINDA smiled; nor was it day before!

Leonard Welsted.

The sun, a radiant lustre holds a while;
The image of ZELINDA's gleamy smile.
A feeble shine does on the water play
And disappear, by turns; a fickle ray.

'ZELINDA wept; when soon the changing skies
Grew black with gathering clouds, that westward rise.
Thin-scattered now, the drops, like gems, descend;
Now, with the frequent shower the lilies bend!
'How calm the air! A pleasing stillness reigns;
And the moist verdure brightens through the plains.
Soft-sinking falls the silver rain; when, lo!
Athwart th' horizon stretched, the Wat'ry Bow
Swells its proud arch, with braided colours gay,
That interchange their dyes, and swift decay.
  The clouds disperse. The sun pursues on high
His vaulted course; and glows along the sky.
The linnets in the dewy bushes sing;
And every field is redolent of Spring!

'Such was the morn, ZELINDA! May it prove
A happy emblem of AMINTOR's love!
Begun by smiling hopes; but soon o'ercast!
Our jealous fears, like clouds, dispersed at last.
Pensive I hung my head, like drooping flowers;
And tears my bosom dewed, like gentle showers.
But soon with settled joys my soul is blessed;
Thy face, my heaven! in lasting smiles is dressed!
Let fond distrust no more past pains renew!
While thou art kind; AMINTOR will be true!'

Barton Booth.

SWEET are the charms of her I love,
  More fragrant than the damask rose,
Soft as the down of turtle-dove,
  Gentle as wind when ZEPHYR blows,
    Refreshing as descending rains
    To sunburnt climes and thirsty plains.

True as the needle to the Pole,
  Or as the dial to the sun;
Constant as gliding waters roll,
  Whose swelling tides obey the moon;
    From ev'ry other Charmer free,
    My life and love shall follow thee!

The lamb, the flow'ry thyme devours.
  The dam, the tender kid pursues.
Sweet PHILOMEL, in shady bowers
  Of verdant Spring, her note renews.
    All follow what they most admire,
    As I pursue my soul's desire!

Nature must change her beauteous face,
  And vary as the Seasons rise:
As Winter, to the Spring gives place;
  Summer, th' approach of Autumn flies.
    No change on Love the Seasons bring;
    Love only knows perpetual Spring!

Barton Booth.

Devouring Time, with stealing pace,
  Makes lofty oaks and cedars bow;
And marble towers, and walls of brass,
  In his rude march, he levels low.
    But Time, destroying far and wide,
    LOVE, from the Soul can ne'er divide!

Death only, with his cruel dart,
  The gentle Godhead can remove;
And drive him from the bleeding heart,
  To mingle with the Blessed above;
    Where, known to all his kindred Train,
    He finds a lasting rest from pain.

LOVE, and his Sister fair, the Soul,
  Twin-born, from Heaven together came.
LOVE will the Universe control,
  When dying Seasons lose their name!
    Divine abodes shall own his power,
    When Time and Death shall be no more!

Isabella Conway, Countess of Hertford.

[SAID TO HAVE BEEN WRITTEN BY LADY HERTFORD TO LORD WILLIAM HAMILTON.]

DEAR COLIN! prevent my warm blushes!
  Since how can I speak without pain!
My eyes have oft told you their wishes!
  Ah! can't you their meaning explain?
My Passion would lose by expression;
  And you, too, might cruelly blame!
Then don't you expect a Confession
  Of what is too tender to name!

Since yours is the province of speaking;
  Why should you expect it of me?
Our wishes should be in our keeping,
  Till you tell us, what they should be!
Then, quickly why don't you discover?
  Did your breast feel tortures like mine,
Eyes need not tell over and over
  What I, in my bosom confine!

Lady Mary Wortley Montagu.

THE ANSWER.

Good Madam! when Ladies are willing;
    A man must needs look like a fool!
For me, I would not give a shilling
    For one that is kind out of rule!
At least, you might stay for my offer;
    Not snatch, like Old Maids in despair!
If you've lived to these years, without proffer;
    Your sighs are now lost in the air!

You might leave me to guess by your blushing!
    And not speak the matter so plain!
'Tis ours to pursue, and be pushing!
    'Tis yours to affect a disdain!
That you're in a pitiful taking,
    By all your sweet ogles I see;
But the fruit that will fall without shaking,
    Indeed, is too mellow for me!

Lady Mary Wortley Montagu.

A RECEIPT TO CURE THE VAPOURS.

Written to Lady Irwin.

Why will Delia thus retire,
    And languish life away?
While the sighing crowd admire,
    'Tis too soon for hartshorn tea!

All those dismal looks and fretting
    Cannot Damon's life restore!
Long ago, the worms have eat him;
    You can never see him more!

Once again consult your toilet!
    In the Glass, your face review!
So much weeping soon will spoil it;
    And no Spring your charms renew!

I, like you, was born a woman!
    Well I know what Vapours mean!
The disease, alas! is common!
    Single, we have all the Spleen!

All the Morals that they tell us,
    Never cured the sorrow yet!
Choose, among the Pretty Fellows,
    One of humour, youth, and wit!

Prithee, hear him, every morning,
  At the least an hour or two!
Once again at night returning;
  I believe the dose will do!

THE ADVICE.

CEASE, fond Shepherd! Cease desiring
  What you never must enjoy!
She derides your vain aspiring!
  She, to all your Sex is coy!

Cunning DAMON once pursued her;
  Yet She never would incline!
STREPHON too, as vainly wooed her,
  Though his flocks are more than thine!

At DIANA's shrine, aloud,
  By the zone around her waist,
Thrice She bowed, and thrice She vowed,
  Like the Goddess, to be chaste.

THE ANSWER.

THOUGH I never got possession;
  'Tis a pleasure to adore!
Hope, the wretch's only blessing,
  May, in time, procure me more!

Constant courtship may obtain her,
  Where both wealth and merit fail;
And the lucky minute gain her!
  Fate and fancy must prevail!

At DIANA's shrine, aloud,
  By the bow and by the quiver,
Thrice She bowed, and thrice She vowed,
  Once to love—and that for ever!

AN ANSWER TO A LADY,

WHO ADVISED LADY M. W. MONTAGU TO RETIRE.

You little know the heart, that you advise!
I view this various scene with equal eyes!
In crowded Court, I find myself alone;
And pay my worship to a nobler throne!

Long since, the value of this World I knew!
Pitied the folly; and despised the shew!
Well as I can, my tedious part I bear;
And wait dismissal, without pain, or fear!

Seldom I mark Mankind's detested ways;
Not hearing censure, or affecting praise!
And, unconcerned, my future fate I trust
To that sole Being, merciful and just!

Anonymous.

THE VICAR OF BRAY.

In good King Charles's golden days,
  When loyalty no harm meant;
A furious High Churchman I was,
  And so I gained preferment.
Unto my flock I daily preached,
  'Kings are by GOD appointed;
And damned are those, who dare resist,
  Or touch, the Lord's Anointed!'
    And this is law, I will maintain
      Unto my dying day, Sir!
    That whatsoever King shall reign,
      I will be Vicar of Bray, Sir!

When royal James possessed the crown,
  And Popery grew in fashion!
The Penal Law I hooted down;
  And read the *Declaration*!
The Church of Rome, I found would fit
  Full well my constitution;
And I had been a Jesuit
  But for the Revolution.
    And this is law, I will maintain, &c.

Anonymous.

When WILLIAM, our Deliverer, came
  To heal the nation's grievance;
I turned the cat in pan again,
  And swore to him allegiance.
Old principles I did revoke;
  Set conscience at a distance!
Passive Obedience is a joke!
  A jest is Non Resistance!
    And this is law, I will maintain, &c.

When glorious ANNE became our Queen,
  The Church of England's glory!
Another face of things was seen;
  And I became a Tory!
Occasional Conformists base,
  I damned; and Moderation!
And thought the Church in danger was,
  From such prevarication.
    And this is law, I will maintain, &c.

When GEORGE, in pudding time, came o'er;
  And Moderate Men looked big, Sir!
My principles I changed once more;
  And so became a Whig, Sir!
And thus preferment I procured
  From our Faith's great Defender;
And, almost every day, abjured
  The Pope, and the Pretender.
    And this is law, I will maintain, &c.

The Illustrious House of Hanover
  And Protestant Succession;
To these, I lustily will swear,
  Whilst they can keep possession!
For in my faith and loyalty,
  I never once will falter;
But GEORGE, my lawful King shall be,
  Except the Times should alter.
    And this is law, I will maintain, &c.

ADVICE TO THE LADIES.

FLY from false Man! DORINDA, fly!
Believe them not! They'll swear and lie!
They're all deceit and perjury!
  They cannot love above a day!
  For if with you they longer stay;
  'Tis but to steal your heart away!
Exchange of hearts for yours, they've none!
For yours, they'll ne'er return their own!
'Tis conquest they design alone!

TO BELINDA.

IN Church, the *Prayer Book* and the fan displayed,
And solemn curtsies, shew the wily Maid;
At Plays, the leering looks and wanton Airs,
And nods and smiles, are fondly meant for snares.
Alas! vain Charmer! you no Lovers get!
There, you seem hypocrite; and here, coquette!

Alexander Pope.

VERSES

TO THE LADY MARY WORTLEY MONTAGU.

[BEFORE THE QUARREL. 1720.]

    IN Beauty, or Wit,
    No mortal, as yet,
To question your empire has dared!
    But men of discerning
    Have thought, that in Learning,
To yield to a Lady was hard!

    Impertinent Schools,
    With musty dull rules,
Have reading to Females denied:
    So Papists refuse
    The *Bible* to use;
Lest flocks should be wise as their guide!

Alexander Pope.

'Twas a woman, at first
(Indeed she was cursed!),
In Knowledge that tasted delight!
And Sages agree,
The laws should decree
To the first possessor the right!

Then bravely, fair Dame!
Renew the old claim,
Which to your whole Sex does belong!
And let men receive
From a second bright EVE,
The knowledge of Right and Wrong!

But if the first EVE,
Hard doom did receive,
When only one apple had she;
What a punishment new
Shall be found out for you;
Who, tasting, have robbed the whole tree!

Lady Mary W. Montagu, & John, Lord Hervey.

VERSES

ADDRESSED TO [ALEXANDER POPE,] THE IMITATOR OF THE FIRST SATIRE OF THE SECOND BOOK OF HORACE.

[AFTER THE QUARREL. 1733.]

In two large columns on thy motley page,
Where Roman wit is striped with English rage;
Where Ribaldry to Satire makes pretence,
And modern Scandal rolls with ancient Sense:
Whilst on one side, we see how HORACE thought;
And on the other, how he never wrote!
Who can believe, who view the bad and good,
That the dull Copyist better understood
That Spirit he pretends to imitate,
Than heretofore that Greek he did translate!
  Thine is just such an image of *his* pen,
As thou thyself art, of the sons of men!
Where our own species in burlesque we trace,
A Sign-Post likeness of the noble race;
That is at once resemblance and disgrace!
  HORACE can laugh, is delicate, is clear;
You only coarsely rail, or darkly sneer!
His style is elegant, his diction pure;
Whilst none, thy crabbed Numbers can endure,
Hard as thy heart, and as thy birth obscure!

Lady Mary W. Montagu, & John, Lord Hervey.

If he has thorns; they all on roses grow!
Thine, like rude thistles and mean brambles show;
With this exception, that, though rank the soil,
Weeds as they are, they seem produced by toil!
  Satire should, like a polished razor keen,
Wound with a touch that's scarcely felt or seen!
Thine is an oyster-knife, that hacks and hews!
The rage, but not the talent, of abuse! . . .
Neither to Folly, nor to Vice, confined;
The object of thy spleen is Human Kind!
It preys on all! who yield; or who resist!
To thee, 'tis provocation to exist!
  But if thou seest[1] a great and generous heart;
Thy bow is doubly bent to force a dart!
Not only justice vainly we demand;
But even benefits can't rein thy hand!
To this, or that, alike in vain we trust;
Nor find thee less ungrateful than unjust!
  Not even Youth and Beauty can control
The universal rancour of thy Soul!
Charms that might soften Superstition's rage!
Might humble Pride! or thaw the ice of Age!
But how shouldst thou by Beauty's force be moved?
No more for loving made, than to be loved!
It was the equity of righteous Heaven,
That such a Soul, to such a Form was given;
And shews the uniformity of Fate,
That one so odious, should be born to hate!
  When GOD created thee, one would believe

[1] See *Taste*, an Epistle.

Lady Mary W. Montagu, & John, Lord Hervey.

He said the same as to the snake, of Eve.
'To Human Race antipathy declare!
Betwixt them and thee be everlasting war!'
But, O, the sequel of the sentence dread!
And whilst you bruise their heel, beware your head!
  Nor think thy weakness shall be thy defence!
(The female Scold's protection in offence!)
Sure, 'tis as fair to beat who cannot fight,
As 'tis to libel those who cannot write!
And if thou draw'st thy pen, to aid the law;
Others a cudgel, or a rod, may draw!
  If none, with vengeance yet thy crimes pursue,
Or give thy manifold affronts their due;
If limbs unbroken, skin without a stain,
Unwhipped, unblanketed, unkicked, unslain,
That wretched little carcase you retain;
The reason is, not that the World wants eyes;
But thou'rt so mean! They see; and they despise!
  When fretful porcupines, with rancorous will,
From mounted backs shoot forth a harmless quill,
Cool the spectators stand; and, all the while,
Upon the angry little monster smile!
Thus 'tis with thee! whilst impotently safe,
You strike unwounding; we unhurt can laugh!
Who but must laugh, this bully when he sees;
A little insect shiv'ring at a breeze!
One overmatched by ev'ry blast of wind,
Insulting and provoking all Mankind!
  Is this, the Thing to keep Mankind in awe?
To make those 'tremble, who escape the law'?

Lady Mary W. Montagu, & John, Lord Hervey.

Is this, the ridicule to live so long,
The deathless Satire, and immortal Song?
No! Like thy self-blown praise, thy scandal flies;
And, as we're told of wasps, it stings and dies.
  If none do yet return th' intended blow;
You, all your safety to our dullness owe!
But whilst that armour, thy poor corpse defends;
'Twill make thy readers few, as are thy friends!
  Those who thy nature loathed, yet loved thy Art,
Who liked thy head, and yet abhorred thy heart;
Chose thee, to read; but never to converse:
And scorned in Prose, him whom they prized in Verse!
Even they, shall now their partial error see!
Shall shun thy Writings, like thy company!
And to thy books, shall ope their eyes no more
Than to thy person, they would do their door!
  Nor thou the justice of the World disown;
That leaves thee thus, an outcast, and alone!
For though, in Law, to murder be to kill;
In Equity, the murder 's in the will!
Then whilst, with coward hand, you stab a name;
And try, at least, t' assassinate our fame:
Like the first bold Assassin's, be thy lot!
Ne'er be thy guilt forgiven, or forgot!
But as thou hat'st, be hated of Mankind!
And with the emblem of thy crooked mind
Marked on thy back, like CAIN, by GOD's own hand,
Wander like him, accursèd, through the land!

William Bedingfield.

Young Strephon, by his folded sheep,
    Sat wakeful on the plains.
Love held his weary eyes from sleep;
    While silent in the vale,
    The list'ning nightingale
Forgot her own, to hear his strains.

And now the beauteous Queen of Night,
    Unclouded and serene,
Sheds on the neighbouring sea her light.
The neighbouring sea was calm and bright.
The Shepherd sung inspired, and blessed the lovely scene.

'While the sky and seas are shining;
    See, my Flora's charms they wear!
Secret Night, my joys divining,
    Pleased my amorous tale to hear,
    Smiles; and softly turns her Sphere!
While the sky and seas are shining;
    See, my Flora's charms they wear!'

Ah! foolish Shepherd! change thy strain!
    The lovely scene, false joys inspires!
For look, thou fond deluded Swain!
Arising storms invade the Main;
    The Planet of the night,
    Inconstant, from thy sight

Behind a cloud retires!
FLORA is fled! Thou lov'st in vain!
Ah! foolish STREPHON! change thy strain!

  Hope beguiling,
Like the morn and ocean smiling,
 Does thy easy faith betray!
  FLORA ranging,
Like the morn and ocean changing,
 More inconstant proves than they!

APOLLO AND DAPHNE.

DAPHNE, the beautiful and coy,
Along the winding shore of Peneus flew,
 To shun Love's tender offered joy;
Though 'twas a God that did her charms pursue:
While thus APOLLO, in a moving strain,
Awaked his lyre; and softly breathed his amorous pain.

'Fairest mortal! stay and hear!
 Cannot Love with Music joined
 Touch thy unrelenting mind!
Turn thee! Leave thy trembling fear!
Fairest mortal! stay and hear!'
The river's echoing banks, with pleasure did prolong
The sweetly measured sounds; and murmured with
 a Song.

William Bedingfield.

Daphne fled swifter, in despair,
  To shun the God's embrace;
  And to the Genius of the place,
She sighed this wondrous prayer.

'Father Peneus! hear me! aid me!
Let some sudden change invade me!
  Fix me rooted on thy shore!
Cease, Apollo! to persuade me!
  I am Daphne now no more!'

Apollo wond'ring stood, to see
  The Nymph transformed into a tree!
Vain were his lyre, his voice, his tuneful art,
  His Passion, and his race divine!
Nor could th' eternal beams, that round his temples shine,
  Melt the cold Virgin's frozen heart!

Nature alone can love inspire!
Art is vain to move desire!
  If Nature does the Fair incline,
  To their own Passion they'll resign!
Nature alone can love inspire!
Art is vain to move desire!

John Gay.

THE SONG OF POLYPHEMUS.

O, RUDDIER than the cherry!
O, sweeter than the berry!
    O, Nymph more bright
    Than moonshine night!
Like kidlings blithe and merry!

Ripe as the melting cluster!
No lily has such lustre!
    Yet hard to tame
    As raging flame;
And fierce as storms that bluster!

THE POET AND THE ROSE.

'Go, rose, my CHLOE's bosom grace!
  How happy should I prove,
Might I supply that envied place
  With never-fading love!
There, Phœnix-like, beneath her eye,
Involved in fragrance, burn and die!

'Know, hapless flower! that thou shalt find
  More fragrant roses there!
I see thy with'ring head reclined
  With envy and despair!
One common fate we both must prove!
You die, with envy; I, with love!'

John Gay.

SWEET WILLIAM'S FAREWELL
TO BLACK-EYED SUSAN.

ALL in the Downs the Fleet was moored,
   The streamers waving in the wind,
When black-eyed SUSAN came aboard.
   'O, where shall I my True Love find?
Tell me, ye jovial sailors! tell me true,
If my sweet WILLIAM sails among the crew?'

WILLIAM, who, high upon the yard,
   Rocked with the billow to and fro,
Soon as her well-known voice he heard,
   He sighed, and cast his eyes below.
The cord slides swiftly through his glowing hands;
And, quick as lightning, on the deck he stands.

So the sweet lark, high poised in air,
   Shuts close his pinions to his breast
(If, chance, his mate's shrill call he hear),
   And drops at once into her nest.
The noblest Captain in the British Fleet
Might envy WILLIAM's lip, those kisses sweet!

John Gay.

'O, SUSAN! SUSAN! lovely Dear!
  My vows shall ever true remain!
Let me kiss off that falling tear;
  We only part to meet again!
Change as ye list, ye winds! my heart shall be
The faithful compass, that still points to thee!

'Believe not what the landmen say!
  Who tempt with doubts thy constant mind.
They'll tell thee, "Sailors, when away,
  In ev'ry port a Mistress find!"
Yes! Yes! believe them, when they tell thee so;
For thou art present wheresoe'er I go!

'If to far India's coast we sail,
  Thy eyes are seen in di'monds bright!
Thy breath is Afric's spicy gale!
  Thy skin is ivory so white!
Thus ev'ry beauteous object that I view,
Wakes in my soul some charm of lovely SUE!

'Though battle call me from thy arms;
  Let not my pretty SUSAN mourn!'
Though cannons roar; yet, safe from harms,
  WILLIAM shall to his Dear return!
LOVE turns aside the balls that round me fly,
Lest precious tears should drop from SUSAN's eye!'

John Gay.

The Boatswain gave the dreadful word:
   The sails their spreading bosom spread.
No longer must she stay aboard.
   They kissed. She sighed. He hung his head.
Her lessening boat unwilling rows to land.
'Adieu!' she cries; and waved her lily hand.

'Twas when the seas were roaring
   With hollow blasts of wind,
A Damsel lay deploring,
   All on a rock reclined.
Wide o'er the rolling billows
   She cast a wistful look;
Her head was crowned with willows
   That tremble o'er the brook.

'Twelve months are gone and over,
   And nine long tedious days;
Why didst thou, vent'rous Lover!
   Why didst thou trust the seas?
Cease, cease, thou cruel ocean!
   And let my Lover rest!
Ah! what's thy troubled motion
   To that within my breast?

'The merchant, robbed of pleasure,
  Sees tempests in despair;
But what 's the loss of treasure
  To losing of my Dear!
Should you, some coast be laid on,
  Where gold and di'monds grow,
You'd find a richer Maiden;
  But none that loves you so!

'How can they say, That Nature
  Has nothing made in vain?
Why then, beneath the water,
  Should hideous rocks remain?
No eyes the rocks discover,
  That lurk beneath the deep,
To wreck the wand'ring Lover;
  And leave the Maid to weep!'

All melancholy lying,
  Thus wailed She for her Dear;
Repaid each blast with sighing,
  Each billow with a tear.
When, o'er the white wave stooping,
  His floating corpse she spied;
Then, like a lily drooping,
  She bowed her head, and died.

John Gay.

DAPHNIS AND CHLOE.

Daphnis stood pensive in the shade,
  With arms across and head reclined;
Pale looks accused the cruel Maid,
  And sighs relieved his love-sick mind.
His tuneful pipe all broken lay.
Looks, sighs, and actions seemed to say,
    'My Chloe is unkind!'

'Why ring the woods with warbling throats?
  Ye larks, ye linnets, cease your strains!
I faintly hear, in your sweet notes,
  My Chloe's voice, that wakes my pains.
Yet why should you, your song forbear?
Your mates delight your Song to hear;
    But Chloe mine disdains!'

As thus he melancholy stood,
  Dejected as the lonely dove,
Sweet sounds broke gently through the wood.
  'I feel the sound! My heart-strings move!
'Twas not the nightingale that sung!
No! 'Tis my Chloe's sweeter tongue!
    Hark! Hark! What says my Love?'

John Gay.

How foolish is the Nymph, she cries,
  Who trifles with her Lover's pain!
Nature still speaks in Woman's eyes;
  Our artful lips were made to feign!
O, DAPHNIS! DAPHNIS! 'twas my pride!
'Twas not my heart, thy love denied!
  Come back, dear Youth! again!

As t' other day my hand he seized,
  My blood with thrilling motion flew!
Sudden, I put on looks displeased;
  And hasty from his hold withdrew!
'Twas fear alone, thou simple Swain!
Then, hadst thou pressed my hand again,
  My heart had yielded too!

'Tis true, thy tuneful reed I blamed!
  That swelled thy lip and rosy cheek.
Think not thy skill in Song defamed;
  That lip should other pleasures seek!
Much, much, thy music I approve;
Yet break thy pipe! for more I love,
  Much more, to hear thee speak!

My heart forebodes that I'm betrayed!
  DAPHNIS, I fear, is ever gone!
Last night, with DELIA's dog he played.
  Love by such trifles first comes on!
Now, now, dear Shepherd! come away!
My tongue would now my heart obey!
  Ah! CHLOE! thou art won!

The Youth stepped forth, with hasty pace,
  And found where wishing CHLOE lay.
Shame sudden lightened in her face;
  Confused, she knew not what to say.
At last, in broken words, she cried,
To morrow, you, in vain, had tried;
  But I am lost to-day!

MY OWN EPITAPH.

LIFE is a jest; and all things show it!
I thought so once; but, now, I know it!

John Gay.

MOLLY MOG;

OR,

THE FAIR MAID OF THE INN.

Says my uncle, 'I pray you, discover
    What hath been the cause of your woes?
Why you pine, and you whine, like a Lover?'
    'I have seen MOLLY MOG of the *Rose*! . . .

'I know that by Wits 'tis recited,
    "That women, at best, are a clog!"
But I am not so easily frighted
    From loving of sweet MOLLY MOG!

'The Schoolboy's desire is Play Day,
    The Schoolmaster's joy is to flog,
The Milkmaid's delight is on May Day;
    But mine is on sweet MOLLY MOG!

'Will-a-wisp leads the traveller a gadding
    Through ditch, and through quagmire and bog;
But no light can set me a madding,
    Like the eyes of my sweet MOLLY MOG!

'For guineas in other men's breeches,
　　Your Gamesters will palm, and will cog!
But I envy them none of their riches,
　　So I may win sweet MOLLY MOG!

'The heart, when half-wounded, is changing;
　　It here and there leaps like a frog!
But my heart can never be ranging,
　　'Tis so fixed upon sweet MOLLY MOG!

'Who follows all Ladies of Pleasure,
　　In pleasure is thought but a hog!
All the Sex cannot give so good measure
　　Of joys as my sweet MOLLY MOG!

'I feel, I'm in love to distraction!
　　My senses all lost in a fog!
And nothing can give satisfaction
　　But thinking of sweet MOLLY MOG!

'A letter when I am inditing,
　　Comes CUPID, and gives me a jog!
And I fill all the paper with writing
　　Of nothing but sweet MOLLY MOG!

John Gay.

'If I would not give up the three Graces;
  I wish I were hanged like a dog!
And at Court, all the Drawing Room faces;
  For a glance of my sweet MOLLY MOG!

'Those faces want nature and spirit,
  And seem as cut out of a log!
JUNO's, VENUS', and PALLAS' merit
  Unite in my sweet MOLLY MOG!

'Those who toast all the Family Royal
  In bumpers of HOGAN and NOG,
Have hearts not more true, or more loyal,
  Than mine to my sweet MOLLY MOG.

'Were VIRGIL alive, with his PHILLIS,
  And writing another Eclogue,
Both his PHILLIS and fair AMARYLLIS
  He'd give up for sweet MOLLY MOG!

'When she smiles on each guest, like her liquor,
  Then jealousy sets me agog!
To be sure, she's a bit for the Vicar;
  And so I shall lose MOLLY MOG!'

John Gay.

SONGS FROM 'THE BEGGAR'S OPERA.'

Youth 's the season made for joys!
Love is then our duty!
She alone who that employs,
Well deserves her beauty!
Let 's be gay,
While we may!
Beauty 's a flower, despised in decay!
CHORUS. Youth 's the season made for joys! &c.

Let us drink and sport to-day!
Ours is not to-morrow!
Love, with Youth, flies swift away!
Age is nought but sorrow!
Dance and sing!
Time 's on the wing!
Life never knows the return of Spring!
CHORUS. Let us drink and sport to-day! &c.

MACHEATH'S SONG.

How happy could I be with either,
Were t' other dear Charmer away!
But while you thus tease me together;
To neither a word will I say!
But tol de rol, tol de rol, &c.

John Gay.

Polly's Song.

Cease your funning!
Force, or cunning,
Never shall my heart trepan!
All these sallies
Are but malice,
To seduce my constant man!
'Tis most certain,
By their flirting,
Women oft have envy shown;
Pleased to ruin
Others' wooing;
Never happy in their own!

Lockit's Song.

When you censure the Age,
Be cautious and sage;
Lest the Courtiers offended should be!
If you mention Vice, or Bribe,
'Tis so pat to all the tribe,
Each cries, 'That was levelled at me!'

Thomas Tickell.

COLIN AND LUCY.

OF Leinster, famed for Maidens fair,
  Bright LUCY was the Grace;
Nor e'er did Liffey's limpid stream
  Reflect a fairer face,
Till luckless love and pining care
  Impaired her rosy hue,
Her dainty lip, her damask cheek,
  And eyes of glossy blue.

Ah! have you seen a lily pale,
  When beating rains descend?
So drooped this slow-consuming Maid,
  Her life now near its end.
By LUCY warned; of flattering Swains
  Take heed, ye easy Fair!
Of vengeance due to broken vows,
  Ye flatt'ring Swains, beware!

Three times, all in the dead of night,
  A bell was heard to ring;
And at her window, shrieking thrice,
  The raven flapped his wing.
Full well the love-lorn Maiden knew
  The solemn boding sound;
And thus, in dying words, bespoke
  The virgins weeping round.

Thomas Tickell.

'I hear a voice, you cannot hear,
  That cries, I must not stay!
I see a hand, you cannot see,
  That beckons me away!
Of a false Swain, and broken heart,
  In early youth I die!
Am I to blame, because the Bride
  Is thrice as rich as I?

'Ah! COLIN! Give not her thy vows!
  Vows due to me alone!
Nor thou, rash Girl! return his kiss;
  Nor think him all thy own!
To-morrow in the Church to wed,
  Impatient both prepare!
But know, false Man! and know, fond Maid!
  Poor LUCY will be there!

'Then bear my corse, ye comrades dear!
  This Bridegroom blithe to meet:
He in his wedding trim so gay;
  I in my winding sheet!'
She spoke. She died. Her corse was borne
  The Bridegroom blithe to meet:
He in his wedding trim so gay;
  She in her winding sheet.

What then were COLIN's dismal thoughts?
   How were these nuptials kept?
The bridesmen flock round LUCY dead,
   And all the village wept.
Confusion, shame, remorse, despair,
   At once his bosom swell:
The damps of death bedewed his brow.
   He groaned. He shook. He fell.

From the vain Bride (a Bride no more!)
   The varying crimson fled,
When, stretched before her rival's corse
   She saw her Lover dead.
He to his LUCY's new-made grave,
   Conveyed by trembling Swains,
In the same mould, beneath one sod,
   For ever now remains.

Oft, at this place, the constant Hind
   And plighted Maid are seen;
With garlands gay, and True-Love Knots,
   To deck the sacred green.
But Swain forsworn, whoe'er thou art!
   This hallowed spot forbear!
Remember COLIN's dreadful fate;
   And fear to meet him there!

Edward Ward.

A SOUTH SEA BALLAD,
OR MERRY REMARKS UPON EXCHANGE ALLEY BUBBLES.

IN London stands a famous Pile,
    And near that Pile an Alley;
Where merry crowds for riches toil,
    And Wisdom stoops to Folly.
Here, sad and joyful, high and low,
    Court FORTUNE for her graces;
And as she smiles, or frowns, they show
    Their gestures and grimaces.

Here, Stars and Garters do appear
    Among our lords the rabble;
To buy and sell, to see and hear
    The Jews and Gentiles squabble.
Here, crafty Courtiers are too wise
    For those who trust to FORTUNE!
They see the cheat, with clearer eyes,
    Who peep behind the curtain! . . .

Long Heads may thrive, by sober rules;
    Because they think, and drink not!
But Headlongs are our thriving fools;
    Who only drink, and think not!
The lucky rogues, like spaniel dogs,
    Leap into South Sea water;
And there they fish for golden frogs;
    Not caring what comes after.

Edward Ward.

'Tis said, that alchemists of old
   Could turn a brazen kettle,
Or leaden cistern, into gold;
   That noble tempting metal.
But (if it here may be allowed,
   To bring in great with small things)
Our cunning South Sea, like a God,
   Turns Nothing into All Things!

What need have we of Indian wealth,
   Or commerce with our neighbours!
Our Constitution is in health;
   And riches crown our labours!
Our South Sea ships have golden shrouds!
   They bring us wealth, 'tis granted:
But lodge their treasure in the clouds,
   To hide it, till it's wanted!

O, Britain! bless thy present state!
   Thou only happy nation!
So oddly rich, so madly great,
   Since Bubbles came in fashion!
Successful Rakes exert their pride,
   And count their airy millions;
Whilst homely Drabs, in coaches ride,
   Brought up to Town on pillions.

Edward Ward.

Few men who follow Reason's rules,
  Grow fat with South Sea diet!
Young Rattles and unthinking fools
  Are those that flourish by it!
Old musty Jades, and pushing Blades,
  Who've least consideration,
Grow rich apace; while wiser heads
  Are struck with admiration.

A race of men, who, t' other day,
  Lay crushed beneath disasters,
Are now, by Stock, brought into play;
  And made our lords and masters.
But should our South Sea Babel fall,
  What numbers would be frowning!
The losers then must ease their gall
  By hanging, or by drowning!

Five Hundred Millions, Notes and Bonds,
  Our Stocks are worth in value:
But neither lie in goods, or lands,
  Or money, let me tell ye!
Yet though our foreign trade is lost;
  Of mighty wealth we vapour!
When all the riches that we boast
  Consist of scraps of paper!

Anonymous.

WILLIAM AND MARGARET.

An old Ballad.

When all was wrapped in dark midnight,
   And all were fast asleep;
In glided Margaret's grimly ghost,
   And stood at William's feet.

Her face was like the April morn
   Clad in a wintry cloud;
And clay-cold was her lily hand,
   That held the sable shroud.

So shall the fairest face appear,
   When youth and years are flown;
Such is the robe that Kings must wear,
   When Death has reft their crown.

Her bloom was like the springing flower,
   That sips the silver dew;
The rose was budded in her cheek,
   And opening to the view:

But Love had, like the canker worm,
   Consumed her early prime;
The rose grew pale, and left her cheek.
   She died before her time!

Anonymous.

'Awake!' she cried, 'thy True Love calls!
    Come from her midnight grave;
Now, let thy pity hear the Maid,
    Thy love refused to save!

'This is the mirk and fearful hour,
    When injured ghosts complain;
And dreary graves give up their dead,
    To haunt the faithless Swain.

'Bethink thee, WILLIAM! of thy fault,
    Thy pledge, and broken oath!
And give me back my maiden vow;
    And give me back my troth!

'How could you say, my face was fair;
    And yet that face forsake?
How could you win my virgin heart;
    Yet leave that heart to break?

'How could you promise love to me;
    And not that promise keep?
Why did you swear, mine eyes were bright;
    Yet leave those eyes to weep?

'How could you say, my lip was sweet,
    And made the scarlet pale?
And why did I, young witless Maid!
    Believe the flattering tale?

Anonymous.

'That face, alas! no more is fair;
   These lips, no longer red;
Dark are mine eyes, now closed in death;
   And every charm is fled!

'The hungry worm, my sister is!
   This winding sheet I wear!
And cold and weary lasts our night,
   Till that at Last Morn appear!

'But, hark! The cock has warned me hence!
   A long and last Adieu!
Come, see, false man! how low she lies,
   That died for love of you!'

Now, birds did sing, and Morning smile
   And shew her glistening head;
Pale WILLIAM shook in ev'ry limb;
   Then, raving, left his bed.

He hied him to the fatal place,
   Where MARGARET's body lay;
And stretched him on the green grass turf,
   That wrapped her breathless clay.

And thrice he called on MARGARET's name!
   And thrice he wept full sore!
Then laid his cheek to the cold earth;
   And word spake never more.

Allan Ramsay.

Give me a Lass with a lump of land;
   And we, for life, shall gang together!
Foolish, or wise, I'll ne'er demand!
   Or black, or white, it makes not whether!

I'm off with Wit! and Beauty will fade!
   And Blood alone is not worth a shilling!
But she that's rich, her market's made;
   For ev'ry charm about her is killing!

Give me a Lass with a lump of land;
   And, in my bosom, I'll hug my treasure!
If I had once her gold in my hand;
   Should love turn dead, it will find pleasure!

Laugh on who likes; but there's my hand!
   I hate, with poortith, though bonny, to meddle!
Unless they bring cash, or a lump of land;
   They'se never get me to dance to their fiddle!

There's meikle good love in bands and bags!
   And silver and gold's a sweet complexion!
But Beauty, and Wit, and Virtue, in rags,
   Have lost the art of gaining affection!

Love tips his arrows with woods and parks,
   And castles, and riggs, and moors, and meadows;
And nothing can catch our modern Sparks
   But well-tochered Lasses, or jointured Widows!

Allan Ramsay.

BONNY CHRISTY.

'How sweetly smells the simmer green!
    Sweet taste the peach and cherry!
Painting and Order please our een;
    And Claret makes us merry!
But finest colours, fruits, and flowers,
    And wine, though I be thirsty,
Lose a' their charms and weaker powers
    Compared with those of CHRISTY!

'When wand'ring o'er the flow'ry Park,
    No nat'ral beauty wanting;
How lightsome is 't to hear the lark,
    And birds in consort chanting!
But if my CHRISTY tunes her voice,
    I'm rapt in admiration!
My thoughts with ecstasies rejoice,
    And drap the hale creation!

'Whene'er she smiles a kindly glance,
    I take the happy omen;
And aften mint to make advance,
    Hoping she'll prove a woman:
But, dubious of my ain desert,
    My sentiments I smother:
With secret sighs I vex my heart,
    For fear she love another.'

Allan Ramsay.

Thus sang blate EDIE by a burn.
 His CHRISTY did o'erhear him:
She doughtna let her Lover mourn;
 But, ere he wist, drew near him.
She spake her favour with a look,
 Which left nae room to doubt her.
He wisely his white minute took;
 And flang his arms about her.

'My CHRISTY! Witness, bonny stream!
 Sic joys frae tears arising!
I wish this may na be a dream!
 O, love the maist surprising!'
Time was too precious now for tauk!
 This point of a' his wishes,
He wadna with set speeches bauk;
 But wair'd it a' on kisses.

THE POET'S WISH.

Quid dedicatum poscit APOLLINEM
Vates?
 HOR.

'Frae great APOLLO, Poet say,
What is thy wish? What wadst thou hae,
 When thou bows at his shrine?'
Not Carse o' Gowrie's fertile field;
Nor a' the flocks the Grampians yield,
 That are baith sleek and fine:

Allan Ramsay.

Not costly things brought frae afar,
  As ivory, pearl, and gems;
Nor those fair Straths, that water'd are
  With Tay and Tweed's smooth streams;
      Which gently and daintily
      Eat down the flow'ry braes,
      As greatly and quietly
      They wimple to the seas.

'Whaever, by his canny fate,
Is master of a good estate,
  That can ilk thing afford,
Let him enjoy 't withoutten care;
And with the wale of curious fare
  Cover his ample board!
Much dawted by the Gods is he,
  Wha to the Indian plain
Successfu' ploughs the wally sea;
  And safe returns again
      With riches, that hitches
      Him high aboon the rest
      Of sma' folk, and a' folk
      That are wi' poortith prest.

'For me, I can be well content
To eat my bannock on the bent,
  And kitchen 't wi' fresh air!
Of lang kail I can make a feast;

And cantily had up my crest,
  And laugh at dishes rare!
Nought frae APOLLO I demand
  But, throw a lengthen'd life,
My outer fabric firm may stand,
  And saul clear without strife!
      May he then but gie then
        Those blessings for my skair;
      I'll fairly and squairly
        Quite a', and seek nae mair!

THE RESPONSE OF THE ORACLE.

To keep thy saul frae puny strife,
And heeze thee out of vulgar life;
  We, in a morning dream,
Whispered Our Will concerning thee
To MARLUS, stretch'd beneath a tree,
  Hard by a poppling stream.
He, full of me, shall point the way,
  Where thou a Star shalt see!
The influence of whose bright ray
  Shall wing thy Muse to flee.
      Mair speer na! and fear na;
        But set thy mind to rest!
      Aspire ay still high'r, ay!
        And always hope the best!

Nicholas Amhurst.

THE TEST OF LOVE.

To a Friend, who fancied himself in love.

Oft hast thou told me, Dick! in friendly part,
That the usurper Love has seized thy heart,
But thou art young! and, like our sanguine race
In their full vigour, mayst mistake thy case!
For, trust me! Love, that inmate of the mind,
Is very much mistaken by Mankind!
For which, too often, is misunderstood
The sudden rage and madness of the blood.
   Thus, every common Rake his flame approves;
And when he's lewd and rampant, thinks he loves!

   But I, who in that study am grown old,
Will to my friend such certain Marks unfold;
By which a real Passion he may prove;
And, without which, he cannot truly love.

   How does this tyrant lord it in thy mind?
What symptoms of his empire dost thou find?
Dost thou within perceive the growing wound?
Does thy soul sicken, while thy body's sound?
Does, in thy thought, some blooming Beauty reign;
Whose strong Idea mingles joy with pain?

Nicholas Amhurst.

When She appears before thee, does She spread
O'er thy pale, fading cheeks, a sudden red?
Press her soft lips, or touch her lilied hand;
Does thy heart flutter? does thy breast expand?
If but her name is mentioned, does it fire
Thy pulses with a quick and fierce desire?
Does every glance, like JOVE's vindictive flame,
Shoot through thy veins, and kindle all thy frame?
    From hence, a real Passion you may prove!
    For he who wants these Symptoms, does not love!

    Is to One woman all your heart inclined?
And can She only charm your constant mind?
For her, do all your morning wishes rise?
Does She, at night, of slumber rob your eyes?
Musing on her, does She alone excite
Your thoughts by day, and all your dreams by night?
Or does your heart for every Nymph you meet,
Own a new Passion, and as strongly beat?
Do, in your eyes, all women seem the same;
And each new face expel the former flame?
    From hence, a real Passion you may prove!
    If you love more than One, you do not love!

    Does Love, and only Love, invade your heart?
Or is it stricken with a golden dart?
Does the keen arrow from her beauty fly?
Or does her fortune glitter in your eye?
For, in this Age, how seldom is it found

Nicholas Amhurst.

That Love alone inflicts the secret wound!
Silver and Gold are CUPID's surest Arms!
One Thousand Pounds outweighs ten thousand charms!
But art thou sure, that in thy tender heart
These worldly baubles bear no sordid part?
And canst thou say, sincerely canst thou say,
Should adverse fortune on thy Charmer prey,
That still unchanged thy Passion would remain?
That still thou wouldst abide a faithful Swain?
If in the cursed South Sea her all were lost,
Still would her eyes, their former conquests boast?
And would She, dost thou think! in every state,
The same emotions in thy soul create?
    From hence, a real Passion you may prove!
    For if you sigh for Wealth, you do not love!

    Again, my friend, incline thy patient ear!
For thou hast many Questions still to hear.
This chosen Damsel, this triumphant She,
Canst thou no blemish in her person see?
Her temper, shape, her features and her Air
(Though never yet was born a faultless Fair!),
Do they all please? In body, or in mind,
Canst thou no blot, nor imperfection, find?
Does o'er her skin no mole, nor pimple, rise;
Or do e'en these seem beauties in thy eyes?
    From hence, a real Passion you may prove!
    For if you spy one Fault, you do not love!

Nicholas Amhurst.

   Do you, within, a sudden impulse feel
To dress, look florid, and appear genteel?
Do you affect to strike the gazing Maid
With glittering gems, with velvet, and brocade?
Your snowy wrists, do Mechlin pendants grace;
And do the smartest wigs adorn thy face?
Do you correct your gait, adjust your Air;
And bid your tailor take uncommon care?
Before your Glass, each morning do you stand;
And tie your neck-cloth with a critic's hand?
    From hence, a real Passion you may prove!
    For Dressing ever was a mark of Love!

   Do books and worldly cares no longer please?
Can no diversions give your heart-pains ease?
Have Wealth and Honours lost their wonted charms;
And does Ambition yield to CUPID's Arms?
Is your whole frame dissolved, by Love ingrost,
To Study, Interest, and Preferment lost?
    From hence, a real Passion you may prove!
    For if aught else prevails, you do not love!

   Do all your thoughts, your wishes, and desires,
Comply with her; and burn with mutual fires?
If She loves Balls, Assemblies, Operas, Plays;
Do they, in you the same amusement raise?
If She, at Ombre loves to waste the night;
Do you, in Ombre take the same delight?

Nicholas Amhurst.

If to the Ring, her graceful horses prance;
Does your new chariot to the Ring advance?
If in the Mall, She chooses to appear,
Or if at Court; do you attend her there?
What She commends, does your officious tongue
Approve; and censure what She judges wrong?
Are all her loves, and her aversions, thine?
In all her joys and sorrows dost thou join?
Art thou, my friend! united to her frame;
Thy heart, thy Passions, and thy soul the same?
   From hence, a real Passion you may prove!
   For without Sympathy, you cannot love!

Didst thou e'er strive (once more kindly say!)
With Friends and Wine to drive thy cares away?
And have e'en these endeavours proved in vain?
Will neither Friends, nor Wine, remove thy pain?
Dost thou sit pensive, full of thought, repine;
And, in thy turn, forget the circling Wine?
   From hence, a real Passion you may prove!
   For if Wine drowns your flame, you do not love!

Art thou a tame, resigned, submissive Swain?
Canst thou bear scorn, repulses, and disdain?
Can no ill treatment, nor unkind returns,
Quench the strong flame, which in thy marrow burns?
But do they rather aggravate thy smart;
And give a quicker edge to every dart?

Nicholas Amhurst.

Does not each scornful look, or angry jest,
Drive the keen Passion deeper in thy breast?
Do not her poignant questions and replies,
Thy partial ears agreeably surprise?
   From hence, a real Passion you may prove!
   For if you can resent, you do not love!

   Whole life-long days you have enjoyed her sight;
Say, were your eyes e'er sated with delight?
Did not you wish next moment to return?
Did not your breast with stronger ardours burn?
Did not each view, another view provoke;
And every meeting give a deeper stroke?
   From hence, a real Passion you may prove!
   For there is no Satiety in Love!

   Perhaps, you judge it an imprudent flame;
And therefore live at distance from the Dame.
But what is the effect? Does absence heal
Those wounds which, smarting in her sight you feel?
Does not, to her your mind unbidden stray?
Does not your heart confess her distant sway?
Does not each rising thought enhance your pain;
And don't you long to see her *once again*?
   From hence, a real Passion you may prove!
   For that which Absence cancels, is not Love!

Nicholas Amhurst.

Suppose, once more, your parents, or your friends,
Either for peevish, or prudential, ends,
Should thwart thy choice! thy promised bliss oppose!
Wouldst thou, for her, engage all these thy foes?
Wouldst thou despise an angry father's frown;
And scorn the noisy censures of the Town?
Couldst thou, possessed of her, with patience see
The coxcomb's finger pointed forth at thee?
Would it not vex you, as you pass along,
To hear the little spleen of every tongue?
'There goes the fond young fool; who, t' other day,
In heedless wedlock threw himself away!
And, to indulge the rash ungoverned heat
Of a vain Passion, lost a good estate!'
Would not such insults grate thy tender ear?
Couldst thou, besides, without compunction bear
The scornful smile, and the disdainful sneer?
  From hence, a real Passion you may prove!
  For he who loves with Reason, does not love!

Still must I touch thee in a tenderer part!
Would not a happy rival stab thy heart?
Couldst thou behold the darling of thy breast
With freedom by another Youth carest?
Say, couldst thou, to thy dearest friend, afford
A kiss, a smile, or one obliging word?
Say, at a Public Ball, or Private Dance,
When the brisk Couples artfully advance,
Couldst thou, unmoved with indignation stand,

If to another She resigned her hand?
Would your heart rest at ease? or would it swell
With all the pains, the sharpest pains, of Hell?
  From hence, a real Passion you may prove!
  For without Jealousy, you cannot love!

  To the last Question of thy trusty friend
(Though many more might still be asked!) attend!
To purge her virtue, or revenge her wrongs
(For Beauty is the theme of busy tongues!);
Should blood be called for, in the doubtful strife,
Wouldst thou, with pleasure, part with blood?—or life?
Wouldst thou, all dangers in her Cause despise;
And meet unequal foes, for such a prize?
Would it not plant new courage in thy heart;
And double vigour to thy arm impart?
To screen thy Mistress from the slightest harms;
Wouldst thou not purchase death; and would not
    death have charms?
  From hence, a real Passion you may prove!
  For never yet was Coward known to love!

  By these Prescriptions judge your inward part!
Put all these Questions closely to your heart!
And if, by them, your flame you can approve;
Then will I own, that you sincerely love!

THE BROOM OF COWDENKNOWS.

How blyth, ilk morn, was I to see
    The Swain come o'er the hill!
He skipt the burn, and flew to me;
    I met him with good will!
  O, the broom, the bonny bonny broom,
    The broom of Cowdenknows!
  I wish I were with my dear Swain,
    With his pipe and my ews.

I neither wanted ew nor lamb,
    While his flock near me lay:
He gather'd in my sheep at night;
    And chear'd me a' the day!
  O, the broom, the bonny bonny broom, &c.

He tun'd his pipe and reed sae sweet,
    The birds stood list'ning by:
Even the dull cattle stood and gazed,
    Charm'd with his melody!
  O, the broom, the bonny bonny broom, &c.

While thus we spent our time by turns
    Between our flocks and play;
I envy'd not the fairest Dame,
    Tho' ne'er sae rich and gay!
  O, the broom, the bonny bonny broom, &c.

S. R.

Hard fate! that I shou'd banish'd be,
  Gang heavily and mourn;
Because I lov'd the kindest Swain
  That ever yet was born!
O, the broom, the bonny bonny broom, &c.

He did oblige me ev'ry hour;
  Cou'd I but faithfu' be?
He staw my heart; cou'd I refuse
  Whate'er he ask'd of me?
O, the broom, the bonny bonny broom, &c.

My doggie, and my lettle kit
  That held my wee soup whey,
My plaidy, broach, and crooked stick,
  May now ly useless by!
O, the broom, the bonny bonny broom, &c.

Adieu, ye Cowdenknows! adieu!
  Farewell a' pleasures there!
Ye Gods! restore to me my Swain!
  Is a' I crave, or care.
O, the broom, the bonny bonny broom, &c.

William Hamilton.

'Ye Shepherds of this pleasant vale,
    Where Yarrow streams along,
Forsake your rural toils, and join
    In my triumphant Song!
She grants! She yields! One heavenly smile
    Atones her long delays!
One happy minute crowns the pains
    Of many suff'ring days!

' Raise, raise the victor notes of joy!
    These suff'ring days are o'er!
Love satiates now his boundless wish
    From Beauty's boundless store.
No doubtful hopes, no anxious fears,
    This rising calm destroy!
Now every prospect smiles around,
    All opening into joy!

'The sun with double lustre shone
    That dear consenting hour,
Brightened each hill, and o'er each vale
    New coloured every flower.
The gales, their gentle sighs withheld;
    No leaf was seen to move!
The hov'ring songsters round were mute;
    And wonder hushed the grove!

William Hamilton.

'The hills and dales no more resound
　　The lambkin's tender cry!
Without one murmur, Yarrow stole
　　In dimpling silence by!
All Nature seemed, in still repose,
　　Her voice alone to hear;
That gently rolled the tuneful wave.
　　She spoke, and blessed my ear.

'"Take, take whate'er of bless, or joy,
　　You fondly fancy mine!
Whate'er of joy, or bless, I boast;
　　Love renders wholly thine!"
The woods struck up, to the soft gale;
　　The leaves were seen to move!
The feathered choir resumed their voice;
　　And wonder filled the grove!

'The hills and dales again resound
　　The lambkin's tender cry,
With all his murmurs, Yarrow trilled
　　The Song of Triumph by!
Above, beneath, around, all on
　　Was Verdure, Beauty, Song!
I snatched her to my trembling breast!
　　All Nature joyed along!'

William Hamilton.

'Ye Shepherds and Nymphs, that adorn the gay plain,
Approach from your sports, and attend to my strain!
Amongst all your number, a Lover so true
Was ne'er so undone, with such bliss in his view!

'Was ever a Nymph so hard-hearted as mine!
She knows me sincere; and she sees how I pine!
She does not disdain me, nor frown in her wrath;
But calmly and mildly resigns me to death!

'She calls me her Friend; but her Lover denies!
She smiles, when I'm cheerful; but hears not my sighs!
A bosom so flinty, so gentle an Air,
Inspires me with hope; and yet bids me despair!

'I fall at her feet, and implore her with tears;
Her answer confounds, while her manner endears!
When softly She tells me, to hope no relief;
My trembling lips bless her, in spite of my grief!

'By night, while I slumber still haunted with care,
I start up in anguish, and sigh for the Fair!
The Fair sleeps in peace! May She ever do so;
And only when dreaming imagine my woe!'

'Then, gaze at a distance; nor further aspire!
Nor think She should love, whom She cannot admire!
Hush all thy complaining; and, dying her slave,
Commend her to Heaven, thyself to the grave!'

Rev. Samuel Wesley.

WHAT man, in his wits, had not rather be poor,
    Than for lucre his freedom to give!
Ever busy the means of his life to secure;
    And so ever neglecting to live!

Invironed from morning to night in a crowd;
    Not a moment unbent, or alone!
Constrained to be abject, though never so proud;
    And at every one's call but his own!

Still repining, and longing for quiet, each hour;
    Yet studiously flying it still!
With the means of enjoying his wish, in his power;
    But accursed with his wanting the will!

For a year must be past, or a day must be come,
    Before he has leisure to rest;
He must add to his store, this, or that, pretty sum;
    And then will have time to be blest!

But his gains, more bewitching the more they increase,
    Only swell the desire of his eye!
Such a wretch, let mine enemy live, if he please!
    Let not even mine enemy die!

PHILLIS is lively, brisk, and gay;
    And loves the crystal springs,
Where she, with Fountain Nymphs does play;
    And to DIANA sings.

She roves through sweet ambrosial bowers,
    And meekly lives at ease.
She culls, in groves, the sweetest flowers;
    And has no Swain to please!

CUPID STRINGING HIS BOW
IN AN IDALIAN MEAD.

  HERE, CUPID puffed, and strung his bow;
Resolved the Nymphs his power should know.
DRUSILLA, this can testify!
  For as the Nymph stood peeping by;
Because she could not hold, but smile
To see the Chit of VENUS toil,
The Boy, forsooth, offended grew;
And, at her breast, his arrow flew,
As, in the mead, the Virgin lay,
She did a heaven of charms display.
  To view her wound, bright VENUS grieved,
And, in her pain, the Nymph relieved;
Then vowed, by Styx! she'd CUPID bind,
If to the Maid he proved unkind.

THE BEE.

A WANTON Bee, of ancient fame,
From Hybla's mountain singing came;
And, pleased, he flies through ev'ry field,
Where daffs and kingcups odours yield;
But lighting on VIRENIA's arm,
When Sleep to rest her eyes did charm,
He finer sweets does gather there;
Nor would he to his hive repair.
  The waking Nymph, surprised to see
Th' unusual fondness of the Bee,
War to denounce she was afraid,
And chose to form an ambuscade.
To him a sprig of thyme did shove,
A herb that every Bee does love.
But he of this no notice took;
At which, with fear the Virgin shook:
When, by indulgent JUNO sent,
A Fountain Nymph to help her went.
The sportive Bee then flew away;
And bright VIRENIA gained the day.

Lady Grissel Baillie.

There was an a May, and she lo'ed na men,
She bigged her bonny bow'r down in yon Glen:
But now she cryes, 'Dale and a well-a-day!
Come down the Green gate, and come here away!

'When bonny young Johnny came o'er the sea,
He said, He saw nathing so bonny as me.
He haight me baith rings and mony bra things:
And were ne my heart 's light, I wad dye!

'He had a wee Titty that lo'ed na me;
Because I was twice as bonny as She!
She rais'd sick a pother 'twixt him and his mother,
That were ne my heart 's light, I wad dye!

'The day it was set, and the Bridal to be,
The Wife took a dwalm, and lay down to dye;
She main'd and She grain'd, out of dollor and pain,
Till he vowed, That he ne'er wou'd see me again!

'His kin was for ane of a higher degree,
Said, "What had he do with the likes of me?
Appose I was bonny, I was ne for Johnny!"
And were ne my heart 's light, I wad dye!

Lady Grissel Baillie.

'They said, "I had neither cow nor calf,
Nor drops of drink runs thro' the drawf,
Nor pickles of meal runs thro' the Mill Eye."
And were ne my heart's light, I wad dye!

'The Maiden she was baith willy and slye.
She spyed me, as I came o'er the Lee;
And then she ran in, and made sick a din!
Beleive your ain een, an ye trow ne me!

'His bonnet stood ay fu' round on his brow,
His auld ane lookt ay as well as his new:
But now, he lets 't gang any gate it will hing;
And casts himsell down on the corn bing.

'And now, he gaes drooping about the dykes;
And a' he dow do, is to hund the tykes.
The live-lang night he ne'er bows his eye:
And were ne my heart's light, I wad dye!

'But young for thee as I ha' been,
We shou'd ha' been galloping down in yon Green;
And linking out o'er yon lilly-white Lee:
And wow gin I were young for thee.'

Matthew Concanen.

THE ADVICE.

The Lass that would know how to manage a man;
    Let her listen, and learn it from me!
His courage to quail, or his heart to trepan,
    As time and occasions agree.

The Girl that has beauty, though small be her wit,
    May wheedle the Clown, or the Beau;
The Rake may repel; or may draw in the Cit,
    By the use of that pretty word 'No!'

When the powdered toupees, in crowds round her chat,
    Each striving his Passion to show;
With 'Kiss me!' and 'Love me, my Dear!' and all that;
    Let her answer be still, 'No! No! No!'

When a dose is contrived to lay virtue asleep,
    A present, a treat, or a Ball!
She still must refuse, if her empire she'd keep;
    And 'No!' be her answer to all!

But when Master Dapperwit offers his hand,
    Her partner in wedlock to go;
A house, and a coach, and a jointure in land;
    She's an idiot, if then she says 'No!'

Matthew Concanen.

Whene'er she 's attacked by a Youth full of charms,
    Whose courtship proclaims him a Man;
When pressed to his bosom, and clasped in his arms,
    Then, let her say 'No,' if she can!

THE THEFT.

WHY are those charms by frowns disgraced,
    Too lovely, and too coy!
Since from your lips, with tim'rous haste,
    I snatched transporting joy?

Too well I rue the hapless theft!
    Too fatal your disdain!
I lost—Ah! no! My life is left,
    I feel it by the pain!

Sure, might I taste another such,
    So warm with keen desire,
My soul, exulting at the touch,
    Would, through my lips, expire!

Then, JULIA! take my parting breath
    In such another kiss!
Glut your revenge! and let my death
    Atone the ravished bliss!

Richard Savage.

VERSES

TO A YOUNG LADY.

   POLLY! from me, though now a love-sick Youth,
Nay, though a Poet, hear the voice of truth!
   POLLY! you're not a Beauty; yet you're pretty!
So grave, yet gay! so silly, yet so witty!
A heart of softness, yet a tongue of satire!
You've cruelty; yet, e'en with that, good nature!
Now you are free, and now reserved a while!
Now a forced frown betrays a willing smile!
Reproached for absence, yet your sight denied;
My tongue you silence, yet my silence chide!
How would you praise me! should your Sex defame;
Yet, should they praise, grow jealous and exclaim!
If I despair, with some kind look you bless;
But if I hope, at once all hope suppress!
You scorn! yet should my Passion change, or fail;
Too late, you'd whimper out a softer tale!
You love! yet from your Lover's wish retire;
Doubt, yet discern! deny, and yet desire!
   Such, POLLY! are your Sex! Part truth, part fiction;
Some thought, much whim, and all a contradiction!

THE GENTLEMAN.

ADDRESSED TO JOHN JOLIFFE, ESQUIRE.

A DECENT mien, an elegance of dress;
Words which, at ease, each winning grace express.
A life where Love, by Wisdom polished, shines;
Where Wisdom's self again, by Love, refines.
A mind where Pity, Mirth, and Friendship reign.
A nature ever great, and never vain.
A wit that no licentious pertness knows;
The sense that unassuming Candour shows.
A love of Learning, knowledge of mankind,
Meekness unservile, and a taste refined.
Unwilling censure; yet a judgement clear.
A smile indulgent, and a soul sincere.
  If these, esteem and admiration raise;
If where these live, they form a living praise:
In one bright view, th' Accomplished Man we see!
These virtues all are thine; and thou art He!

Anonymous.

Away! Let nought to Love displeasing,
　My Winifreda! move your care!
Let nought delay the heavenly blessing;
　Nor squeamish pride, nor gloomy fear!

What though no grants of royal donors,
　With pompous titles grace our blood:
We'll shine in more substantial honours;
　And to be noble, we'll be good!

Our name, while Virtue thus we tender,
　Will sweetly sound where'er 'tis spoke:
And all the Great Ones, they shall wonder
　How they respect such little folk!

What though from Fortune's lavish bounty,
　No mighty treasures we possess:
We'll find, within our pittance, plenty;
　And be content, without excess!

Still shall each kind returning season
　Sufficient for our wishes give:
For we will live a life of reason,
　And that's the only life to live!

Through youth and age, in love excelling,
　We'll hand in hand together tread!
Sweet-smiling Peace shall crown our dwelling;
　And babes, sweet-smiling babes, our bed!

How should I love the pretty creatures,
  While round my knees they fondly clung!
To see them look their mother's features;
  To hear them lisp their mother's tongue!

And when, with envy Time transported,
  Shall think to rob us of our joys;
You'll, in your Girls, again be courted;
  And I'll go wooing in my Boys!

ON THE SETTING UP OF MR. SAMUEL BUTLER'S MONUMENT IN WESTMINSTER ABBEY.

WHILE BUTLER, needy wretch! was yet alive,
No gen'rous Patron would a dinner give!
See him, when starved to death and turned to dust,
Presented with a monumental bust!
The Poet's fate is here in emblem shown:
He asked for bread, and he received a stone!

EPITAPH ON TOM D'URFEY.

HERE lies the Lyric, who, with Tale and Song,
Did life to threescore years and ten prolong.
His Tale was pleasant, and his Song was sweet,
His heart was cheerful—but his thirst was great!
Grieve, Reader! grieve that he, too soon grown old,
His Song has ended, and his Tale has told.

Dean Jonathan Swift.

ADVICE

TO THE GRUB STREET VERSE WRITERS.

Written in the year 1726.

YE Poets ragged and forlorn,
   Down from your garrets haste!
Ye Rhymers, dead as soon as born,
   Not yet consigned to paste!

I know a trick to make you thrive!
   O, 'tis a quaint device!
Your still-born Poems shall revive,
   And scorn to wrap up spice!

Get all your verses printed fair,
   Then, let them well be dried;
And CURLL must have a special care
   To leave the margin wide.

Lend these to paper-sparing POPE!
   And, when he sets to write,
No letter with an envelope
   Could give him more delight!

When POPE has filled the margins round;
   Why then, recall your loan!
Sell them to CURLL for Fifty Pound;
   And swear they are your own!

Dean Jonathan Swift.

TO MR. POPE,

WHILE HE WAS WRITING 'THE DUNCIAD.'

Written in the year 1726.

Pope has the talent well to speak;
    But not to reach the ear.
His loudest voice is low and weak;
    The Dean too deaf to hear.

A while they on each other look,
    Then diff'rent studies choose;
The Dean sits plodding on a book,
    Pope walks, and courts the Muse.

Now packs of letters, though designed
    For those who more will need them,
Are filled with hints, and interlined;
    Himself can hardly read them!

Each atom, by some other struck,
    All turns and motions tries;
Till, in a lump together stuck,
    Behold a Poem rise!

Yet to the Dean his share allot!
    He claims it by a Canon,
'That without which a thing is not,
    Is *causa sine qua non.*'

Thus, POPE! in vain, you boast your wit!
   For had our deaf Divine
Been for your conversation fit,
   You had not writ a line!

Of SHERLOCK thus, for preaching famed,
   The Sexton reasoned well;
And justly half the merit claimed,
   Because he *rang the Bell.*

MARY THE COOK-MAID'S LETTER

TO [THE REV.] DOCTOR SHERIDAN.

Written in the year 1723.

WELL! if ever I saw such another man, since my mother bound my head!
You, a Gentleman! Marry, come up! I wonder, where you were bred?
I am sure, such words do not become a Man of your Cloth!
I would not give such language to a dog! faith and troth!
Yes! You called my Master 'a Knave!' Fie! Mr. SHERIDAN! 'tis a shame
For a Parson, who should know better things, to come out with such a name!
'Knave' in your teeth, Mr. SHERIDAN! 'Tis both a shame and a sin;
And the Dean, my Master, is an honester man than you and all your kin!
He has more goodness in his little finger, than you have in your whole
   body!
My Master is a parsonable man; and not a spindle-shanked hoddy-
   doddy!
And now whereby I find you would fain make an excuse,
Because my Master, one day, in anger, called you 'Goose!'
Which, and I am sure I have been his servant four years since October,
And he never called me worse than 'Sweet-heart!', drunk or sober.

Dean Jonathan Swift.

Not that I know that his Reverence was ever concerned, to my knowledge;
Though you and your come-rogues keep him out so late, in your wicked College.
You say, 'You will eat grass on his grave!' A Christian eat grass!
Whereby you now confess yourself to be a goose, or an ass.
But that 's as much as to say, That my Master should die before ye!
Well! Well! That 's as God pleases! and I don't believe that 's a true story!
And so say, I told you so! and you may go tell my Master! What care I!
And I don't care who knows it! 'Tis all one to MARY!
Everybody knows that I love to tell truth, and shame the Devil!
I am but a poor servant; but I think Gentlefolks should be civil!

Besides, you found fault with our vittels, one day that you were here;
I remember it was upon a Tuesday, of all days in the year!
And SAUNDERS, the Man, says, You are always jesting and mocking.
'MARY,' said he, one day, as I was mending my Master's stocking,
'My Master is so fond of that Minister, that keeps the School!
I thought my Master was a wise man; but that man makes him a fool!'
'SAUNDERS,' says I, 'I would rather than a quart of ale,
He would come into our kitchen; and I would pin a dish-clout to his tail!'

And now, I must go, and get SAUNDERS to direct this letter!
For I write but a sad scrawl! but my sister MARGET, she writes better.
Well! but I must run, and make the bed, before my Master comes from Prayers.
And see now, it strikes ten! and I hear him coming upstairs.
Whereof I could say more to your Verses, if I could write written hand:
And so I remain, in a civil way, Your servant to command,

                                                         MARY.

William Somervile.

A SONG FOR THE LUTE.

Gently, my Lute! move ev'ry string!
  Soft as my sighs, reveal my pain!
While I, in plaintive Numbers sing
  Of slighted vows, and cold disdain.

In vain, her Airs! in vain, her art!
  In vain, she frowns when I appear!
Thy notes shall melt her frozen heart!
  She cannot hate, if She can hear!

And see, She smiles! Through all the groves
  Triumphant *Iö Peans* sound!
Clap all your wings, ye little Loves!
  Ye sportive Graces, dance around!

Ye list'ning oaks, bend to my Song!
  Not Orpheus played a nobler Lay!
Ye savages, about me throng!
  Ye rocks, and harder hearts, obey!

She comes! She comes! relenting Fair!
  To fill with joy my longing arms.
What faithful Lover can despair,
  Who thus with Verse and Music charms!

William Somervile.

A HUNTING SONG.

BEHOLD, my friend! the rosy-fingered Morn,
    With blushes on her face,
        Peeps o'er yon azure hill!
        Rich gems, the trees enchase!
        Pearls from each bush distil!
Arise! Arise! and hail the light new-born!

Hark! Hark! The merry horn calls, 'Come away!'
    Quit, quit thy downy bed!
        Break from AMYNTA's arms!
        O, let it ne'er be said
        That all, that all her charms
(Though she 's as VENUS fair!) can tempt thy stay!

Perplex thy soul no more with cares below!
    For what will pelf avail?
        Thy courser paws the ground,
        Each beagle cocks his tail,
        They spend their months around;
While health and pleasure smile on every brow!

William Somervile.

Try, Huntsmen! all the brakes! spread all the plain!
    Now, now, she 's gone away!
        Strip! Strip! with speed pursue!
    The jocund God of Day,
        Who fain our sport would view,
See! See! he flogs his fiery steeds in vain!

Pour down, like a flood from the hills, brave Boys!
    On the wings of the wind,
        The merry beagles fly!
    Dull Sorrow lags behind!
        Ye shrill echoes, reply!
Catch each flying sound; and double our joys!

Ye rocks, woods, and caves, our music repeat!
    The bright Spheres thus above,
        A gay refulgent Train,
    Harmoniously move,
        O'er yon celestial plain,
Like us, whirl along in concert so sweet!

Now Puss threads the brakes, and heavily flies!
    At the head of the pack
        Old Fidler bears the bell!
    Every foil he hunts back,
        And aloud rings her knell;
Till forced into view, she pants, and she dies!

William Somervile.

In Life's dull round, thus we toil and we sweat!
    Diseases, Grief, and Pain,
      An implacable crew,
    While we double in vain,
      Unrelenting pursue;
Till, quite hunted down, we yield with regret.

This moment is ours! Come, live while ye may!
    What 's decreed by dark Fate
      Is not in our own power!
    Since To-morrow 's too late,
      Take the present kind hour!
With Wine cheer the night; as Sports bless the day!

Edward Roome.

SONGS FROM 'THE JOVIAL CREW,'
1731.

SHE was not coy!
She would laugh and toy;
Yet preserved her virgin fame!
She was her father's only joy;
And every Shepherd's flame.
Though many strove,
Yet none could move,
Till STREPHON, young and gay,
Inspired her soul with virtuous love;
And stole her heart away!

THOUGH women, 'tis true, are but tender;
Yet Nature does strength supply!
Their will is too strong to surrender!
They're obstinate still, till they die!
In vain, you attack them with reason;
Your sorrows you only prolong!
Disputing is always High Treason;
No woman was e'er in the wrong!
Your only relief is to bear!
And when you appear content,
Perhaps, in compassion, the Fair
May persuade herself into consent!

Edward Roome.

THE mind of a woman can never be known!
    You never can guess it aright!
I'll tell you the reason!—She knows not her own;
    It changes so often ere night!
        'Twould puzzle APOLLO,
        Her whimseys to follow;
His oracle would be a jest!
She'll frown, when she 's kind;
Then, quickly you'll find
She'll change with the wind;
      And often abuses
      The man that she chooses;
    And what she refuses,
        Likes best!

THERE was an old fellow at Waltham Cross,
Who merrily sung, when he lived by the loss!
He cheered up his heart, when his goods went to rack,
With a 'Hem! Boys! Hem!' and a cup of old Sack.

Edward Roome.

At night, by moonlight, on the plain,
　With rapture have I seen,
Attended by her harmless Train,
　The little Fairy Queen,
Her midnight Revels sweetly keep!
While mortals are involved in sleep,
　They tripped it o'er the Green!

And where they danced their cheerful Round,
　The morning would disclose!
For where their nimble feet do bound,
　Each flower unbidden grows!
The daisy, fair as Maids in May,
The cowslip, in his gold array,
　And blushing violet, 'rose!

　'Did our sighing Lovers know
What a pain we undergo;
Sweeter would their wooing prove!
Shorter were the way to Love!
Unkind commands, when they obey,
We suffer more, much more, than they!
And to rebel, were kinder still;
Than to obey (against our will)!'

Mary Barber.

STELLA AND FLAVIA.

STELLA and FLAVIA, ev'ry hour,
  Unnumbered hearts surprise.
In STELLA's soul lies all her power;
  And FLAVIA's, in her eyes.

More boundless FLAVIA's conquests are;
  And STELLA's more confined.
All can discern a face that 's fair;
  But few, a lovely mind.

STELLA, like Britain's Monarch, reigns
  O'er cultivated lands:
Like Eastern tyrants, FLAVIA deigns
  To rule o'er barren sands.

Then boast, fair FLAVIA! boast your face!
  Your beauty's only store.
Your charms will ev'ry day decrease!
  Each day gives STELLA more!

THE COBBLER'S END.

A Cobbler there was, and he lived in a stall;
Which served him for Parlour, for Kitchen, and Hall.
No coin in his pocket, nor care in his pate;
No ambition had he, nor duns at his gate.
    Derry down, down, down, derry down.

Contented he worked, and he thought himself happy,
If, at night, he could purchase a jug of brown Nappy.
He'd laugh then, and whistle, and sing too most sweet,
Saying, 'Just to a hair, I've made both ends meet!'
    Derry down, down, down, derry down.

But Love, the disturber of high and of low,
That shoots at the Peasant as well as the Beau,
He shot the poor Cobbler quite through the heart!
I wish he had hit some more ignoble part!
    Derry down, down, down, derry down.

It was from a cellar this archer did play,
Where a buxom young damsel continually lay.
Her eyes shone so bright, when she rose every day,
That she shot the poor Cobbler, quite over the way.
    Derry down, down, down, derry down.

Anonymous.

He sang her Love Songs, as he sat at his work;
But she was as hard as a Jew, or a Turk.
Whenever he spake, she would flounce and would fleer;
Which put the poor Cobbler quite into despair.
    Derry down, down, down, derry down.

He took up his *awl* that he had in the world;
And to make away with himself was resolved!
He pierced through his body, instead of the *sole*.
So the Cobbler he died; and the bell it did toll.
    Derry down, down, down, derry down.

And now, in good will, I advise as a friend,
All Cobblers take warning by this Cobbler's *end*!
Keep your hearts out of love! for we find, by what's past,
That love brings us *awl* to an *end* at the *last*.
    Derry down, down, down, derry down.

THE LONDON LASS.

WHAT though I am a London Dame,
    And lofty looks I bear a;
I carry, sure, as good a name
    As those who russet wear a!
What though my clothes are rich brocade;
    My skin it is more white a
Than any of the Country Maids,
    That in the field delight a!

Anonymous.

What though I to Assemblies go,
   And at the Opera shine a;
It is a thing all Girls must do,
   That will be Ladies fine a!
And while I hear FAUSTINA sing
   Before the King and Queen a;
My eyes, they are upon the wing,
   To see if I am seen a!

My Pekoe and Imperial Tea
   Are brought me in the Morn a;
At Noon, Champagne and rich Tokay,
   My tables do adorn a;
The Evening then does me invite
   To play at dear Quadrille a:
And, sure, in this, there's more delight
   Than in a purling rill a!

Then, since my fortune does allow
   Me to live as I please a;
I'll never milk my father's cow,
   Nor press his coming cheese a!
But take my swing, both night and day;
   I'm sure it is no sin a!
And as for what the grave ones say,
   I value not a pin a!

Charles Mordaunt, Earl of Peterborough.

I SAID to my heart, between sleeping and waking,
'Thou wild thing! that always art leaping, or aching!
What Black, Brown, or Fair, in what clime, in what
 nation,
By turns has not taught thee a pit-a-pat-ation?'

Thus accused; the wild thing gave this sober reply:
'See the heart without motion, though CŒLIA pass by!
Not the beauty she has, nor the wit that she borrows,
Gives the eye any joys, or the heart any sorrows!

'When our SAPPHO appears, she whose wit so refined
I am forced to applaud with the rest of mankind,
Whatever she says is with spirit and fire!
Ev'ry word I attend; but I only admire!

'PRUDENTIA as vainly would put in her claim;
Ever gazing on heaven, though Man is her aim.
'Tis Love, not Devotion, that turns up her eyes!
Those stars of this world are too good for the skies!

'But CLOE so lively, so easy, so fair!
Her wit so genteel, without art, without care!
When she comes in my way, the motion, the pain,
The leapings, the achings, return all again!'

O, wonderful creature! a woman of reason!
Never grave out of pride; never gay out of season!
When so easy to guess, who this angel should be,
Would one think Mrs. HOWARD ne'er dreamt it was she?

Joseph Thurston.

CONSTANCY.

How firmly fixed, I thought my heart,
    When PHYLLIS first I knew;
So deep the wound, so sharp the dart,
    I must be ever true!

Such dazzling charms her glances shot!
    Her eyes, such pointed rays!
I sighed; and wished it were my lot
    Eternally to gaze!

Long did I serve the gentle Dame,
    Pine, languish, and adore!
Till, on a time, PASTORA came;
    And PHYLLIS was no more!

PASTORA seized my heart with joy;
    Small cause had she to boast!
For, soon, the restless wand'ring toy
    Was to BELINDA lost!

I thought BELINDA was divine,
    So fair, so gay, so young!
BELINDA! I had still been thine;
    If CHLOE had not sung!

For BELVIDERA, next, I bled;
  And wooed her with my tears!
Till DELIA took me, in her stead;
  And AMORET, in hers!

Like me, ye Swains! your time improve;
  And Woman's pride will fall!
Be never true to One in love;
  But constant to them All!

ON A LADY'S FAN.

I SLYLY stole this secret Charm,
In hopes my CHLOE to disarm.
The artifice was mean and poor;
And she as potent as before!
  Let JOVE, his thunder lay aside;
His Godhead soon will be defied!
If VENUS but her Zone remove;
You would not know the Queen of Love!
And CUPID, maugre all his skill,
Without his bow, could never kill!
  Fair Nymph! thy boundless power I own
Dependent on thyself alone!
Superior thou, in every part,
Alike to Nature, as to Art!

Anonymous.

A HEALTH TO ALL HONEST MEN!

EVERY man take his Glass in his hand;
   And drink a Good Health to our King!
Many years may he rule o'er this land!
   May his laurels for ever fresh spring!
Let wrangling and jangling straightway cease!
Let every man strive for his country's peace!
     Neither Tory, nor Whig,
     With their Parties, look big!
Here 's a Health to all honest men!

'Tis not owning a whimsical name
   That proves a man loyal and just!
Let him fight for his country's fame!
   Be impartial at home, if in trust!
'Tis this, that proves him an honest soul!
His Health we'll drink in a brimful bowl!
     Then let 's leave off debate!
     No confusion create!
Here 's a Health to all honest men!

When a company 's honestly met,
   With intent to be merry and gay,
Their drooping spirits to whet,
   And drown the fatigues of the day;
What madness is it, thus to dispute,
When neither Side can his man confute!

When you've said what you dare,
  You're but just where you were!
Here 's a Health to all honest men!

Then agree, ye true Britons! agree!
  And ne'er quarrel about a nickname!
Let your enemies trembling see
  That an Englishman 's always the same!
For our King, our Church, our laws, and right;
Let 's lay by all feuds, and straight unite!
    Then who need care a fig
    Who 's a Tory, or Whig!
Here 's a Health to all honest men!

VERSES

WRITTEN ON ONE OF THE WINDOWS OF DOCTOR DELANY'S HOUSE AT DELVILLE.

A BARD, grown desirous of saving his pelf,
Built a house he was sure would hold none but himself.
This enraged God APOLLO, who MERCURY sent,
And bid him go ask, What his Votary meant?
  'Some foe to my empire has been his adviser;
'Tis of dreadful portent when a Poet turns miser!
Tell him, HERMES, from me! tell that subject of mine!
I have sworn, by the Styx! to defeat his design!
For, wherever he lives, the Muses shall reign;
And the Muses, he knows, have a numerous Train.'

THE DECLAIMER.

'Woman! thoughtless, giddy creature!
   Laughing, idle, flutt'ring thing!
Most fantastic work of Nature!
   Still, like Fancy, on the wing!

'Slave to ev'ry changing Passion;
   Loving, hating, in extreme!
Fond of ev'ry foolish fashion;
   And, at best, a pleasing dream!

'Lovely trifle! dear illusion!
   Conqu'ring weakness! wished-for pain!
Man's chief glory, and confusion!
   Of all vanity most vain!'

Thus deriding Beauty's power,
   Bevil called it all a cheat!
But, in less than half an hour,
   Kneeled, and whined, at Celia's feet!

Henry Baker, F.R.S.

THE MODISH LOVER.

WITH downcast eyes and folded arms,
    Young MYRTLE sauntered out one day,
Reflecting on FLORINDA's charms,
    The fair, the blooming, and the gay.
Deeply he sighed, his bosom all aflame;
And on the dust, he flourished out her name.

Next morn, abroad he walked again;
    Much altered since the day before.
A good night's rest had cured his pain;
    Nor was FLORINDA thought of more.
But giddy Chance, the fickle Youth had brought
Close by that spot, where he her name had wrote.

The place recalls to mind his flame;
    When, all in love, he wandered there.
''Twas here,' he cries, 'I left the name
    Of yesterday's commanding Fair!'
Pensive a while he stood; then looked to find
What beauteous image had possessed his mind.

But vain, alas, his searches prove.
    The rain had fallen, the wind had blown;
And, sympathizing with his love,
    Away was ev'ry letter flown!
Nor could his faithless memory declare
Whose name he, yesterday, had flourished there!

DAMON AND CHLOE.

DAMON. Love 's an idle childish Passion,
  Only fit for girls and boys!
Marriage is a cursèd fashion!
  Women are but foolish toys!
Spite of all the tempting evils,
  Still thy liberty maintain!
Tell them, tell the pretty Devils!
  'Man alone was made to reign!'

CHLOE. Empty boaster! know thy duty!
  Thou who dar'st my power defy,
Feel the force of Love and Beauty!
  Tremble at my feet, and die!
Wherefore does thy colour leave thee?
  Why these cares upon thy brow?
Did the rebel, Pride, deceive thee?
  Ask him, 'Who 's the Monarch now?'

Anonymous.

ON THE CHOICE OF A WIFE.
SILVIO AND STREPHON.

'IF thou hadst liberty to choose
For life, dear Stripling! let thy Muse,'
Thus SILVIO, to his STREPHON said,
'Give me a picture of the Maid,
With whom you'd live! for whom could die!'
Thus gentle STREPHON made reply.

'Were I, my friend! to choose a Wife,
A dear companion for my life;
A Nymph, my happiest choice should be,
From artifice and falsehood free.
Her education, birth, estate,
Neither too humble, nor too great.

'Wealth should not my affections move.
The treasure I require is Love!
For, surely, riches in excess
Are not the means to happiness!
Yet may kind Heaven sufficient give,
With comfort and with ease to live!

'Beauty alone, I would despise;
Vermilion cheeks and sparkling eyes.
A set of features will decay,
And moulder to their parent-clay:

Yet may the Graces charms impart,
To soothe my eye, and warm my heart!
Charms that may my affections tie,
Till TIME himself grow old, and die!

'She should, devout in constant prayer,
Religion make her chiefest care!
And, next to Heaven, me learn to please,
Crowning my happy days with ease!
Still kind, and kind to me alone!
Her years proportioned to my own.
Her humour of a piece with mine.
Her dress genteelly neat, not fine.
Her temper amiably mild;
With constancy and sweetness filled.

'She should not want the foreign aid
Of silk, embroid'ry, or brocade;
In native innocence arrayed.
Should be with wit and sense endowed,
Yet not of those endowments proud;
Nor stiffly dumb, nor pertly loud.
To decent cheerfulness inclined;
And of the softest mould her mind.
With such a Nymph contented I
Could live! for such a Nymph could die!'

'Whate'er we meet with in Romances,
Or dreaming Lovers' airy fancies;

Surely, such Nymph on British ground,'
Quoth Silvio smiling, 'ne'er was found!'

'O, Silvio!' Strephon sighing said,
'O, did you know the charming Maid!
Had you the fair Eliza viewed,
So chaste, so amiably good,
She's more (with wonder you'd confess!)
Than you can think; or I express!
  'Prudence does o'er her wit preside;
And Reason, all her Passions guide.
Modesty dwells upon her cheek.
The Graces, in her language speak.
Beauty sits on her face confest.
Virtue, with no ill thoughts opprest,
Serenes her brow, and calms her breast.
  'How shall my feeble pencil paint
Her charms, where all description's faint!
O, she has charms enough to move
A hermit's frozen heart to love!
She is adorned with sweetness, ease,
Good nature, every art to please!
From prud'ry, or coquetry, free;
All Man could wish, or Woman be!

  'If I'm indulged to choose a Wife,
A dear companion for my life;
Bless me, kind Heaven! with such a Dame!
And yet not *such*—but O, the *same*!'

THE WHEEDLER.

In vain, dear Cloe! you suggest,
That I, inconstant, have possest
  Or loved a fairer She!
Would you, with ease, at once be cured
Of all the ills you've long endured;
  Consult your Glass and me!

If then, you think that I can find
A Nymph more fair, or one more kind;
  You've reason for your fears!
But if impartial you will prove
To your own beauty and my love;
  How needless are your tears!

If, in my way, I should, by chance,
Receive, or give, a wanton glance;
  I like but while I view!
How slight the glance, how faint the kiss,
Compared to that substantial bliss
  Which I receive from you!

Rt. Hon. Sir William Yonge, Bart.

With wanton flight, the curious bee
From flower to flower still wanders free;
   And, where each blossom blows,
Extracts the juice of all he meets:
But for his quintessence of sweets,
   He ravishes the rose!

So, my fond fancy to employ
On each variety of joy,
   From Nymph to Nymph I roam;
Perhaps, see fifty in a day!
Those are but visits which I pay;
   For CLOE is my home!

George Granville, Lord Lansdowne.

LOVING AT FIRST SIGHT.

No warning of th' approaching flame!
Swiftly, like sudden death, it came!
Like travellers by lightning killed,
I burnt, the moment I beheld!

In whom so many charms are placed,
Is with a mind as nobly graced!
The Case, so shining to behold,
Is filled with richest gems and gold.

To what my eyes admired before,
I add a thousand graces more!
And Fancy blows into a flame
The spark that from her Beauty came!

The object thus improved by thought;
By my own image I am caught!
PYGMALION so, with fatal art,
Polished the Form that stung his heart!

WARNED, and made wise by others' flame;
I fled from whence such mischiefs came.
Shunning the Sex, that kills at sight;
I sought my safety in my flight.

George Granville, Lord Lansdowne.

But, ah! in vain, from Fate we fly!
For, first or last, as all must die;
So 'tis as much decreed above,
That, first or last, we all must love!

My heart, which stood so long the shock
Of winds and waves, like some firm rock,
By one bright spark from MYRA thrown,
Is into flames, like powder, blown!

'FOOLISH LOVE! be gone!' said I,
  'Vain are thy attempts on me!
Thy soft allurements I defy!
Women, those fair dissemblers, fly!
  My heart was never made for thee!'

LOVE heard; and straight prepared a dart.
  'MYRA! revenge my cause!' said he.
Too sure 'twas shot! I feel the smart!
It rends my brain, and tears my heart!
  'O, LOVE! my conqu'ror! pity me!'

'I'LL tell her, the next time!' said I,
  In vain! in vain! for when I try,
Upon my tim'rous tongue the trembling accents die!
  Alas! a thousand thousand fears
    Still overawe, when she appears! [in tears!
My breath is spent in sighs; my eyes are drowned

George Granville, Lord Lansdowne.

THYRSIS AND DELIA.

THYRSIS. DELIA! how long must I despair,
  And tax you with disdain?
 Still to my tender love severe;
  Untouched, when I complain!

DELIA. *When men of equal merit love us,*
  And do with equal ardour sue;
 THYRSIS! you know but one must move us!
  Can I be yours, and STREPHON's, too?

 My eyes view both with mighty pleasure,
  Impartial to your high desert.
 To both alike, esteem I measure!
  To one alone, can give my heart!

THYRSIS. Mysterious Guide of Inclination!
  Tell me, Tyrant! why am I,
 With equal merit, equal Passion,
  Thus the victim chosen to die?
  Why am I
 The victim chosen to die?

George Granville, Lord Lansdowne.

DELIA. On Fate alone depends success;
    And Fancy, Reason overrules!
  Or why should Virtue ever miss
    Reward, so often given to fools?

'Tis not the valiant, nor the witty;
    But who alone is born to please!
Love does predestinate our pity!
    We choose but whom he first decrees!

WHY should a heart so tender break?
    O, MYRA! give its anguish ease!
The use of Beauty you mistake!
    Not meant to vex; but please!

Those lips, for smiling were designed!
    That bosom, to be prest!
Your eyes, to languish, and look kind!
    For amorous arms, your waist!

Each thing has its appointed right,
    Established by the Powers above;
The sun, to give us warmth and light!
    MYRA, to kindle love!

Charles Hamilton, Lord Binning.

A PASTORAL BALLAD.

Did ever Swain, a Nymph adore,
  As I ungrateful Nanny do!
Was ever Shepherd's heart so sore!
  Was ever broken heart so true!
    My eyes are swelled with tears; but she
    Has never shed a tear for me!

If Nanny called, did Robin stay!
  Or linger, when she bid me run!
She only had the word to say;
  And all she asked was quickly done!
    I always thought on her; but she
    Would ne'er bestow a thought on me!

To let her cows my clover taste,
  Have I not rose by break of day!
When did her heifers ever fast,
  If Robin in his yard had hay!
    Though to my fields they welcome were;
    I never welcome was to her!

If Nanny ever lost a sheep,
  I cheerfully did give her two!
Did not her lambs in safety sleep
  Within my folds, in frost and snow!
    Have they not there from cold been free;
    But Nanny still is cold to me!

Charles Hamilton, Lord Binning.

Whene'er I climbed our orchard trees,
  The ripest fruit was kept for NAN!
O, how those hands that drowned her bees
  Were stung! I'll ne'er forget the pain!
    Sweet were the combs, as sweet could be;
    But NANNY ne'er looked sweet on me!

If NANNY to the well did come,
  'Twas I that did her pitchers fill!
Full as they were, I brought them home!
  Her corn I carried to the Mill!
    My back did bear her sacks; but she
    Would never bear the sight of me!

To NANNY's poultry, oats I gave;
  I'm sure, they always had the best!
Within this week, her pigeons have
  Eat up a peck of peas at least!
    Her little pigeons kiss; but she
    Would never take a kiss from me!

Must ROBIN always NANNY woo;
  And NANNY still on ROBIN frown?
Alas, poor wretch! What shall I do?
  If NANNY does not love me soon,
    If no relief to me she'll bring;
    I'll hang me in her apron-string!

George Lyttelton, Lord Lyttelton.

Written in the year 1732.

WHEN DELIA on the plain appears,
Awed by a thousand tender fears,
I would approach; but dare not move!
Tell me, my heart! if this be Love?

Whene'er she speaks, my ravished ear
No other voice but hers can hear!
No other wit but hers approve!
Tell me, my heart! if this be Love?

If she, some other Youth commend,
Though I was once his fondest friend,
His instant enemy I prove!
Tell me, my heart! if this be Love?

When she is absent, I no more
Delight in all that pleased before,
The clearest spring, or shadiest grove!
Tell me, my heart! if this be Love?

When fond of power, of beauty vain,
Her nets she spread for ev'ry Swain;
I strove to hate, but vainly strove!
Tell me, my heart! if this be Love?

George Lyttelton, Lord Lyttelton.

Written in the year 1733.

'THE heavy hours are almost past
    That part my Love and me;
My longing eyes may hope, at last,
    Their only wish to see!

'But how, my DELIA! will you meet
    The man you've lost so long?
Will love in all your pulses beat,
    And tremble on your tongue?

'Will you, in ev'ry look, declare
    Your heart is still the same;
And heal each idly-anxious care
    Our fears, in absence frame?

'Thus, DELIA! thus, I paint the scene,
    When shortly we shall meet;
And try what yet remains between
    Of loit'ring time to cheat.

'But if the dream, that soothes my mind,
    Shall false and groundless prove;
If I am doomed, at length to find
    You have forgot to love:

George Lyttelton, Lord Lyttelton.

'All I of VENUS ask is this—
  No more to let us join;
But grant me here, the flatt'ring bliss
  To die, and think you mine!'

Written in the year 1732.

SAY, MYRA! why is gentle Love
  A stranger to that mind,
Which pity and esteem can move?
  Which can be just and kind?

Is it because you fear to share
  The ills that Love molest?
The jealous doubt, the tender care,
  That rack the am'rous breast?

Alas, by some degree of woe,
  We ev'ry bliss must win!
The heart can ne'er a transport know,
  That never feels a pain!

George Lyttelton, Lord Lyttelton.

POEMS

WRITTEN TO MISS LUCY FORTESCUE,

WHO BECAME HIS WIFE.

To him who in an hour must die,
Not swifter seems that hour to fly;
Than slow the minutes seem to me,
Which keep me from the sight of thee.

Not more that trembling wretch would give
Another day, or year, to live;
Than I, to shorten what remains
Of that long hour which thee detains!

O, come to my impatient arms!
O, come, with all thy heavenly charms!
At once to justify, and pay,
The pain I feel from this delay.

To ease my troubled mind of anxious care,
  Last night, the secret casket I explored,
Where all the letters of my absent Fair
  (Her richest treasure!) careful love had stored.

George Lyttelton, Lord Lyttelton.

In ev'ry word, a magic spell I found,
  Of power to charm each busy thought to rest;
Though ev'ry word increased the tender wound
  Of fond desire, still throbbing in my breast.

So to his hoarded gold, the miser steals,
  And loses ev'ry sorrow at the sight:
Yet, wishes still for more; nor ever feels
  Entire contentment, or secure delight!

Ah! should I lose thee, my too lovely Maid!
  Couldst thou forget thy heart was ever mine!
Fear not thy letters should the change upbraid!
  My hand each dear memorial would resign!

Not one kind word shall in my power remain,
  A painful witness of reproach to thee!
And, lest my heart should still their sense retain,
  My heart shall break, to leave thee wholly free!

A PRAYER TO VENUS,

IN HER TEMPLE AT STOWE.

Fair Venus! whose delightful Shrine surveys
  Its front reflected in the silver lake,
These humble off'rings, which thy servant pays,
  Fresh flowers and myrtle wreaths, propitious take!

George Lyttelton, Lord Lyttelton.

If less my love exceeds all other love
  Than Lucy's charms all other charms excel;
Far from my breast, each soothing hope remove;
  And there, let sad despair for ever dwell!

But if my soul is filled with her alone,
  Nor other wish, nor other object, knows;
O, make her, Goddess! make her all my own!
  And give my trembling heart secure repose!

No watchful spies I ask, to guard her charms!
  No walls of brass! no steel-defended door!
Place her but once within my circling arms,
  Love's surest fort; and I will doubt no more!

ON HER PLEADING WANT OF TIME.

On Thames's bank, a gentle Youth
For Lucy sighed, with matchless truth,
  E'en when he sighed in rhyme.
The gentle Maid, his flame returned;
And would, with equal warmth have burned;
  But that she had not time.

Oft he repaired, with eager feet,
In secret shades his Fair to meet
  Beneath th' accustomed lime.
She would have fondly met him there,
And healed with love each tender care;
  But that she had not time.

George Lyttelton, Lord Lyttelton.

'It was not thus, inconstant Maid!
You acted once,' the Shepherd said,
  'When love was in its prime!'
She grieved to hear him thus complain,
And would have writ to ease his pain;
  But that she had not time.

'How can you act so cold a part?
No crime of mine has changed your heart;
  If love be not a crime!
We soon must part, for months! for years!'
She would have answered with her tears;
  But that she had not time!

When I think on your truth; I doubt you no more!
I blame all the fears I gave way to before!
I say to my heart, 'Be at rest; and believe
That whom once she has chosen, she never will leave!'

But, ah! when I think on each ravishing grace
That plays in the smiles of that heavenly face;
My heart beats again! I again apprehend
Some fortunate rival in ev'ry friend!

These painful suspicions, you cannot remove;
Since you neither can lessen your charms, nor my love!
But doubts caused by Passion, you never can blame;
For they are not ill-founded, or you feel the same!

William Popple.

Cupid and Venus jointly strove
　To warm Amintor's heart;
And give him all the joys of Love,
　Unmixed with any smart.

Venus advised, from ev'ry Fair,
　To steal the sweetest Grace.
'No! No!' says Cupid, 'ease your care;
　They meet in Mordaunt's face!'

'Why should those eyes, Florella! wear
　A chilling scorn to me;
Yet ardent gaze on one who ne'er
　Yet felt a sigh for thee?

'Or why, if you are not decreed
　To ease another's pain,
Am I not of my Passion freed;
　Or you, of your disdain?'

'Forbear, fond Youth!' Florella said,
　'And blame not me; but Fate!
You're doomed, alas! (by her betrayed!)
　To love! and I to hate!'

Rev. John Hoadly.

TO CHLOE.

Written on my Birthday, 1734.

The minutes, the hours, the days, and the years,
    That fill up the current of Time,
Neither flowing with hope, neither ebbing with fears,
    Unheeded rolled on to my prime.

In Infancy prattling, in Youth full of play,
    Still pleased with whatever was new;
I bade the old Cripple fly swifter away,
    To o'ertake some gay trifle in view!

But when Chloe, with sweetness and sense in her [look,
    First taught me the lesson of Love;
Then, I counted each step the winged Fugitive took;
    And bade him more leisurely move!

'Stop, Runaway! stop! nor thy journey pursue;
    For Chloe has gi'en me her heart!
To enjoy it, thy years will prove many too few!
    If you make so much haste to depart.'

Still, still he flies on! Still, still let him fly
    Till he's tired, and panting for breath!
My love, both his teeth and his scythe shall defy!
    That can only be conquered by Death!

CHLOE RESOLVED.

As CHLOE on flowers reclined o'er the stream,
She sighed to the breeze, and made COLIN her theme
Though pleasant the stream, and though cooling the breeze,
And the flowers though fragrant; she panted for ease!

The stream, it was fickle, and hasted away!
It kissed the sweet banks; but no longer could stay!
Though beauteous, inconstant! and faithless, though fair!
Ah! COLIN! look in; and behold thyself there!

The breeze, that so sweet on its bosom did play,
Now rose to a tempest, and darkened the day.
As sweet as the breeze, and as loud as the wind,
Such COLIN, when angry; and COLIN, when kind!

The flowers, when gathered, so beauteous and sweet,
Now fade on her bosom, and die at her feet.
So fair in their bloom, and so foul in decay,
Such COLIN, when present; and COLIN, away!

In rage and despair, from the ground she arose;
And from her, the flowers, so faded, she throws!
She weeps in the stream, and she sighs to the wind;
And resolves to drive COLIN quite out of her mind.

But what her resolves, when her COLIN appeared!
The stream it stood still, and no tempest was heard;
The flowers recovered their beautiful hue;
She found, he was kind; and believed, he was true!

Rev. John Hoadly.

FAIR SALLY loved a bonny Sailor.
  With tears, she sent him out to roam;
Young THOMAS, taking leave, did tell her,
  He left with her his heart at home.
She viewed the seas from off the hill;
And, as she turned her spinning wheel,
    Sung of her bonny Sailor!

The wind grew loud, and she grew paler
  To see the weathercock turn round;
When, lo! she spied her bonny Sailor
  Come whistling o'er the fallow ground.
With nimble haste, he leaped the stile;
Fair SALLY met him with a smile,
    And hugged her bonny Sailor.

Fast round the waist he took his SALLY,
  But first around his mouth wiped he;
Like home-bred Spark he could not dally;
  But pressed and kissed her with a glee!
'Through winds, and waves, and dashing rain,'
Said he, 'thy TOM's returned again,
    To bring a heart for SALLY!'

Rev. John Hoadly.

'Welcome!' cried she, ' my constant THOMAS!
    Though out of sight, ne'er out of mind!
The seas, our hearts have parted from us;
    Yet still my thoughts were left behind.
So much my thoughts took TOMMY's part,
That time, nor absence, from my heart
       Could drive my constant THOMAS!'

'This knife, the gift of lovely SALLY!
    Which still I've kept for her dear sake,
A thousand times, in am'rous folly,
    Her name has carved upon the deck.
Again this happy pledge returns,
To show how truly THOMAS burns,
       How truly burns for SALLY!'

'This thimble, thou didst give to SALLY;
    Whene'er I see, I think on you!
Then why should TOM stand shilly, shall I,
    When yonder steeple 's in our view?'
TOM, never to occasion blind,
Now took her in the coming mind;
       And went to Church with SALLY.

Colley Cibber, P.L.

WHAT Woman could do, I have tried, to be free!
   Yet do all I can,
I find I love him! And though he flies me;
   Still, still, he 's the man!
They tell me, 'At once, he to twenty will swear!'
When vows are so sweet; who, the falsehood will fear?
  So, when you have said all you can,
   Still, still, he 's the man!

I caught him once making love to a Maid.
   When to him I ran;
He turned, and he kissed me! Then, who could upbraid
   So civil a man?
The next day, I found, to a third he was kind.
I rated him soundly! He swore, 'I was blind!'
  So, let me do what I can,
   Still, still, he 's the man!

All the World bids me, 'Beware of his art!'
   I do what I can:
But he has taken such hold of my heart,
   I doubt he 's the man!
So sweet are his kisses, his looks are so kind;
He may have his faults: but if I none can find,
  Who can do more than they can?
   Still, still, he 's the man!

THE BLIND BOY.

'O, say, What is that thing called Light?
   Which I can ne'er enjoy.
What is the blessing of the sight?
   O, tell your poor blind boy!

'You talk of wondrous things you see,
   You say, "The sun shines bright!"
I feel him warm; but how can he
   Then make it day, or night?

'My day, or night, myself I make;
   Whene'er I wake, or play:
And could I ever keep awake,
   It would be always day!

'With heavy sighs, I often hear
   You mourn my hopeless woe:
But, sure, with patience I may bear
   A loss I ne'er can know!

'Then, let not what I cannot have,
   My cheer of mind destroy!
Whilst thus I sing, "I am a King;
   Although a poor blind boy!"'

Anonymous.

CUPID AND FORTUNE FALLEN OUT.

Cupid and Fortune long agreed,
  In ties of sacred friendship bound:
Yet what his purposes decreed,
  Her blind mistakes would oft confound.

When thus Love's God, 'I now defy
  Thy fickle arts! thy Power disown!
Goddess! thou'rt blinder far than I;
  I and Mamma will reign alone!

'Thy gawdy gifts, the rich brocade,
  The gilded chariot, smart toupee,
The silver hilt, the untried blade,
  No more Love's enginry shall be!

'E'en Pin Money shall lose its charms,
  Nor more invade the virgin breast!
So you may shut your lavish arms,
  And set your tott'ring Wheel at rest!

'Or if my wounds, in vain, are made,
  Or should my vot'ries prove untrue;
I'd call in Virtue to my aid,
  Not such a termagant as you!'

'That idolizer of your power,
　Strephon! shall rue for this!' she cries;
Then wings it to that happy Bower,
　Which Mira gladdens with her eyes.

Hence, Fortune (Strephon's worst of foes!)
　Labours to cross his eager flame,
To Mira treach'rous favour shows.
　Mira might all her favours claim!

This raised the Nymph to such a height,
　Created in the Swain such fears,
That he could scarce, or speak, or write;
　Much less with Sonnets charm her ears.

The Goddess, hostile in her smiles,
　Having Love's schemes almost undone,
Thus twits him for his baffled wiles,
　'Pray, how goes Mira's business on?

'That's no concern of mine! you'll say:
　Yet if I'm not a party made,
Blind as I am, I'll find a way
　To spoil your whining am'rous trade!'

Anonymous.

In rage, the little God repairs
  Where VIRTUE's sacred Temples rise;
Where VANITY ne'er shows her Airs,
  Nor FLATT'RY comes, full fraught with lies.

He saw the Goddess, heavenly fair,
  Enthroned, with looks sedately wise:
Open SIMPLICITY was there;
  And modest TRUTH, without disguise.

Then, he begins the Case to state,
  Tells STREPHON's faith, and MIRA's charms;
Intreats, she'd the blind Gipsy rate!
  She spoke; and thus his rage disarms.

'If STREPHON, when approved, shall be
  So full of truth without design,
He shall not want a friend in me;
  And MIRA's a known friend of mine!

'Her pity shall more pleasure give
  Than happy rapturous Lovers write!
On which, poor STREPHON yet may live;
  And triumph over FORTUNE's spite.'

Henry Fielding.

THE dusky night rides down the sky,
  And ushers in the morn!
The hounds all join in glorious cry!
  The hunter winds his horn!
    And a hunting we will go!

The wife, around her husband throws
  Her arms, and begs his stay,
'My dear, it rains! and hails! and snows!
  You will not hunt to-day!'
    But a hunting we will go!

'A brushing fox, in yonder wood,
  Secure to find we seek;
For why? I carried, sound and good,
  A cartload there last week.
    And a hunting we will go!'

Away he goes! He flies the rout!
  Their steeds all spur and switch!
Some are thrown in, and some thrown out;
  And some thrown in the ditch.
    But a hunting we will go!

At length, his strength to faintness worn,
  Poor Reynard ceases flight.
Then, hungry, homeward we return,
  To feast away the night.
    Then a drinking we will go!

Fielding and Leveridge.

[April 1734.]

When mighty Roast Beef was the Englishman's food,
It ennobled our hearts, and enrichèd our blood!
Our soldiers were brave, and our Courtiers were good!
    O, the Roast Beef of Old England,
    And Old England's Roast Beef!

Then, Britons! from all nice dainties refrain;
Which effeminate Italy, France, and Spain!
And mighty Roast Beef shall command on the Main!
    O, the Roast Beef of Old England, &c.

RICHARD LEVERIDGE.

[May 1735.]

When mighty Roast Beef was the Englishman's food,
It ennobled our veins, and enrichèd our blood!
Our soldiers were brave, and our Courtiers were good!
    O, the Roast Beef of Old England,
    And Old English Roast Beef!

But since we have learned from all-conquering France,
To eat their ragouts, as well as to dance,
We are fed up with nothing but vain complaisance.
    O, the Roast Beef of Old England, &c.

Richard Leveridge.

Our fathers, of old, were robust, stout, and strong;
And kept open house, with good cheer, all day long,
Which made their plump tenants rejoice in this Song.
    O, the Roast Beef of Old England, &c.

But, now, we are dwindled, to what shall I name!
A sneaking, poor race, half-begotten and tame;
Who sully those honours that once shone in fame.
    O, the Roast Beef of Old England, &c.

When good Queen ELIZABETH sat on the throne,
Ere Coffee, and Tea, and such slip-slops were known;
The World was in terror, if e'er she did frown!
    O, the Roast Beef of Old England, &c.

In those days, if fleets did presume on the Main;
They seldom, or never, returned back again!
As witness, the vaunting Armada of Spain!
    O, the Roast Beef of Old England, &c.

O, then, they had stomachs to eat and to fight;
And when wrongs were a cooking, to do themselves
    right!
But, now, we're a—— I could; but Good-night!
    O, the Roast Beef of Old England, &c.

Richard Leveridge.

The Play of Love is now begun;
And thus the Actions do go on.
Strephon, enamoured, courts the Fair:
She hears him with a careless air,
And smiles to find him in Love's snare.

The Act Tune played; they meet again.
Here, pity moves her for his pain:
Which She evades with some pretence,
And thinks She may with love dispense;
But pants to hear a Man of Sense!

The third approach her Lover makes,
She colours up whene'er he speaks:
But, with feigned slights, still puts him by;
And faintly cries, 'She can't comply!'
Although She gives her heart the lie.

Now the plot rises. He seems shy,
As if some other Fair he'd try;
At which, She swells with spleen and fear,
Lest some more wise his love should share!
Which, yet, no woman e'er can bear!

The last Act now is wrought so high,
That thus it crowns the Lover's joy!
She does no more his Passion shun.
He straight into her arms does run.
The Curtain falls! The Play is done!

Rev. James Miller.

How brimful of Nothing's the life of a Beau!
They've Nothing to think of! They've Nothing to do!
Nor they've Nothing to talk of—for Nothing they know!
   Such, such is the life of a Beau!

For Nothing they rise, but to draw the fresh air!
Spend the morning in Nothing but curling their hair!
And do Nothing all day, but sing, saunter, and stare!
   Such, such is the life of a Beau!

For Nothing, at night, to the Playhouse they crowd!
For to mind Nothing done there, they always are proud;
But to bow, and to grin, and to talk Nothing aloud!
   Such, such is the life of a Beau!

For Nothing, they run to th' Assembly and Ball;
And for Nothing, at cards a fair Partner call:
For they still must be beasted, who've Nothing at all!
   Such, such is the life of a Beau!

For Nothing, on Sundays, at Church they appear;
For they've Nothing to hope; nor they've Nothing to fear!
They can be Nothing nowhere, who Nothing are here!
   Such, such is the life of a Beau!

Henry Carey.

SALLY IN OUR ALLEY.

OF all the Girls that are so smart,
   There 's none like pretty SALLY!
She is the darling of my heart;
   And she lives in our Alley.
There is no Lady in the land
   Is half so sweet as SALLY!
She is the darling of my heart;
   And she lives in our Alley.

Her father, he makes cabbage-nets,
   And through the streets does cry them;
Her mother, she sells laces long,
   To such as please to buy them.
But, sure, such folks could ne'er beget
   So sweet a Girl as SALLY!
She is the darling of my heart;
   And she lives in our Alley.

When she is by, I leave my work
   (I love her so sincerely!),
My master comes, like any Turk,
   And bangs me most severely.
But let him bang his bellyful;
   I'll bear it all for SALLY!
She is the darling of my heart;
   And she lives in our Alley.

Henry Carey.

Of all the days that 's in the week,
    I dearly love but one day!
And that 's the day that comes betwixt
    A Saturday and Monday.
For then I'm dressed, all in my best,
    To walk abroad with SALLY!
She is the darling of my heart;
    And she lives in our Alley.

My master carries me to Church;
    And often I am blamed,
Because I leave him in the lurch
    As soon as Text is named.
I leave the Church, in Sermon time,
    And slink away to SALLY!
She is the darling of my heart;
    And she lives in our Alley.

When Christmas comes about again,
    O, then I shall have money!
I'll hoard it up, and Box and all
    I'll give it to my Honey!
And would it were Ten Thousand Pounds;
    I'd give it all to SALLY!
She is the darling of my heart;
    And she lives in our Alley.

Henry Carey.

My master and the neighbours all,
  Make game of me and SALLY;
And (but for her!) I'd better be
  A slave, and row a galley!
But when my seven long years are out,
  O, then I'll marry Sally!
O, then we'll wed, and then we'll bed;
  But not in our Alley!

HARRY CAREY'S GENERAL REPLY

TO THE LIBELLING GENTRY, WHO ARE ANGRY AT HIS WELFARE.

WITH an honest old friend, and a merry old Song,
And a flask of old Port; let me sit the night long,
And laugh at the malice of those who repine,
That they must swig Porter, while I can drink Wine!

I envy no mortal, though ever so great;
Nor scorn I a wretch, for his low estate!
But what I abhor, and esteem as a curse,
Is poorness of spirit; not poorness in purse!

Then, dare to be generous, dauntless, and gay!
Let 's merrily pass life's remainder away!
Upheld by our friends; we our foes may despise!
For the more we are envied, the higher we rise!

Henry Carey.

A YORKSHIRE SONG.

I AM, in truth, a Country Youth,
    Unused to London fashions;
Yet Virtue guides, and still presides
    O'er all my steps and Passions.
No courtly leer, but all sincere!
    No bribe shall ever blind me!
If you can like a Yorkshire Tike,
    An honest man you'll find me!

Though Envy's tongue, with slander hung,
    Does oft belie our County;
No men on earth boast greater worth;
    Or more extend their bounty!
Our northern breeze, with us agrees;
    And does for business fit us!
In public cares, in Love's affairs,
    With honour we acquit us!

A noble mind is ne'er confined
    To any shire, or nation!
He gains most praise, who best displays
    A gen'rous education!
While rancour rolls in narrow souls,
    By narrow views discerning;
The truly wise will only prize
    Good Manners, Sense, and Learning!

Henry Carey.

THE FINE LADY'S LIFE,

OR

THE THOUGHTS OF AN AMBITIOUS COUNTRY GIRL

ON THE PLEASURES OF THE TOWN.

WHAT though they call me Country Lass;
I read it plainly in my Glass,
That for a Duchess I might pass!
  O, could I see the day!
Would Fortune but attend my call,
At Park, at Play, at Ring, at Ball;
I'd brave the proudest of them all;
  With a 'Stand by! Clear the way!'

Surrounded by a crowd of Beaus,
With smart toupees and powdered clothes;
At rivals I'll turn up my nose!
  O, could I see the day!
I'll dart such glances from these eyes,
Shall make some Lord, or Duke, my prize!
And then, O, how I'll tyrannize;
  With a 'Stand by! Clear the way!'

O, then for ev'ry new delight,
For equipage and diamonds bright,
Quadrille, and Plays, and Balls, all night!
  O, could I see the day!
Of love and joy I'd take my fill!
The tedious hours of life to kill.
In ev'rything I'd have my will;
  With a 'Stand by! Clear the way!'

THE ROMP'S SONG.

O, I'LL have a husband! aye, marry!
For why should I longer tarry
  Than other brisk Girls have done?
For if I stay till I grow grey,
They'll call me Old Maid, and fusty Old Jade!
  So I'll no longer tarry;
  But I'll have a husband! aye, marry!
    If money can buy me one.

My mother, she says 'I'm too coming!'
And still in my ears she is drumming,
  That I such vain thoughts should shun!
My sisters, they cry 'O, fie!' and 'O fie!';
But yet I can see, they're as coming as me!
  So let me have husbands in plenty!
  I'd rather have twenty times twenty
    Than die an Old Maid undone!

Henry Carey.

CAREY'S WISH.

Cursed be the wretch that's bought and sold;
And barters liberty for gold!
For when Election is not free,
In vain, we boast of liberty;
And he who sells his single Right,
Would sell his country, if he might!

When Liberty is put to sale
For wine, for money, or for ale,
The sellers must be abject slaves;
The buyers, vile designing knaves!
A proverb it has been of old,
'The Devil's bought, but to be sold!'

This maxim, in the Statesman's School,
Is always taught, *Divide! and Rule!*
All Parties are to him a joke!
While zealots foam, he fits the yoke!
When men their reason once resume;
'Tis then the Statesman's turn to fume!

Learn, learn, ye Britons! to unite!
Leave off the old exploded Bite;
Henceforth, let Whig and Tory cease,
And turn all Party rage to peace!

[Then follow in the 1729 Text.]

Rouse! and revive your ancient glory!
Unite and drive the World before ye!

[But in the 1731 Text.]

Then shall we see a glorious scene;
And so, GOD save the King and Queen!

Henry Carey.

THE CONFLICT
BETWEEN LOVE AND WINE.

ALONE, by a lonely willow,
  Poor DAMON sighing lay;
The grass was his only pillow,
  Alack! and well-a-day!

I came, with my flask;
  And I gave him drink.
Had it been a whole cask,
  He'd have drunk it, I think.

He danced and he sang,
  And he capered like mad!
And swore, 'He'd have more,
  If more could be had!'

But CELIA, with charms surrounded,
  Came tripping it o'er the plain.
The Shepherd afresh was wounded;
  And all undone again.

He called her, his Goddess! She called him, an ass!
I plied him again with a cherishing Glass.
He laughed at her scorn, and her power he defied;
And vowed his dear Bottle should alone be his Bride!

Henry Carey.

THE EARLIEST TEXTS OF THE NATIONAL ANTHEM.

I. In a folio Volume of engraved Songs called *Harmonica Anglicana*, without date, but published before November 1742; and afterwards increased to two folio Volumes, and published, also without date, but about 1745, under the title of *Thesaurus Musicus*.

A LOYAL SONG,

SUNG AT THE THEATRES ROYAL.

FOR TWO VOICES.

GOD save great GEORGE our King!
Long live our noble King!
  GOD save the King!
Send him victorious,
Happy and glorious,
Long to reign over us,
  GOD save the King!

O, LORD, our GOD, arise!
Scatter our enemies;
  And make them fall!
Confound their politics!
Frustrate their knavish tricks!
On Thee our hopes we fix!
  GOD save us all!

Thy choicest gifts in store,
On GEORGE, be pleased to pour!
  Long may he reign!
May he defend our laws;
And ever give us cause
With heart and voice to sing,
  GOD save the King!

II. The above Anthem was reprinted in the *Gentleman's Magazine* for October 1745, in the Contents Page of which, it is described as:—

GOD save our Lord the King.

A NEW SONG, SET FOR TWO VOICES.

Which wording also occurs in the Contents Page of the *Thesaurus Musicus* above mentioned.

III. In November 1745, when the Young Pretender was marching into England, the Anthem appeared in an engraved musical Half Sheet, with the following additional stanza:—

O, grant that Marshal WADE
May, by Thy mighty aid,
  Victory bring!
May he sedition hush;
And like a torrent rush
Rebellious Scots to crush!
  GOD save the King!

MRS. STUART'S RETIREMENT.

From the Court, to the Cottage convey me away!
For I'm weary of grandeur, and what they call 'gay';
      Where Pride without measure,
      And Pomp without pleasure,
Make life, in a circle of hurry, decay.

Far remote and retired from the noise of the Town;
I'll exchange my brocade for a plain russet gown!
      My friends shall be few,
      But well chosen and true;
And sweet recreation, our evening shall crown!

With a rural repast, a rich banquet to me,
On a mossy green bank, near some shady old tree,
      The river's clear brink
      Shall afford me my drink;
And Temp'rance, my friendly Physician shall be!

Ever calm and serene, with contentment still blest,
Not too giddy with joy, or with sorrow deprest,
      I'll neither invoke,
      Nor repine at. Death's stroke!
But retire from the world, as I would to my rest.

Catharine Cockburn.

'Ah! gaze not on those eyes! Forbear
That soft enchanting voice to hear!
Not looks of basilisks give surer death;
Nor Sirens sing with more destructive breath!

'Fly! if thy freedom thou'dst maintain!
Alas! I feel th' advice is vain!
A heart, whose safety but in flight does lie,
Is far too lost, to have the power to fly!'

Soft kisses may be innocent;
    But, ah! too easy Maid, beware!
Though that is all thy kindness meant;
    'Tis Love's delusive fatal snare!

No Virgin e'er, at first, designed
    Through all the Maze of Love to stray;
But each new path allures her mind,
    Till, wand'ring on, she lose her way!

'Tis easy, ere set out, to stay;
    But who the useful art can teach,
When sliding down a steepy way,
    To stop, before the end we reach?

Keep ever something in thy power,
    Beyond what would thy honour stain!
He will not dare to aim at more,
    Who for small favours sighs in vain!

James Thomson.

If those who live in Shepherd's bower,
  Press not the rich and stately bed;
The new-mown hay and breathing flower
  A softer couch beneath them spread!

If those who sit at Shepherd's board,
  Soothe not their taste by wanton art;
They take what Nature's gifts afford,
  And take it with a cheerful heart!

If those who drain the Shepherd's bowl,
  No high and sparkling wines can boast;
With wholesome cups they cheer the soul,
  And crown them with the village Toast!

If those who join in Shepherd's sport,
  Gay dancing on the daisied mead,
Have not the splendour of a Court;
  Yet Love adorns the merry Round!

Unless with my Amanda blest,
  In vain, I twine the woodbine bower!
Unless to deck her sweeter breast,
  In vain, I wreathe the breathing flower!

Awakened by the genial year,
  In vain, the birds around me sing!
In vain, the fresh'ning fields appear!
  Without my Love, there is no Spring!

James Thomson.

When Britain first, at Heaven's command,
  Arose from out the azure Main,
This was the Charter of the land;
  And guardian Angels sung *this* strain:
    'Rule, Britannia! rule the waves!
    Britons never will be slaves!

'The nations, not so blessed as thee,
  Must, in their turns, to tyrants fall!
While thou shalt flourish great and free,
  The dread and envy of them all!
    Rule, Britannia! rule the waves!' &c.

'Still more majestic shalt thou rise,
  More dreadful, from each foreign stroke;
As the loud blast, that tears the skies,
  Serves but to root thy native oak!
    Rule, Britannia! rule the waves!' &c.

'Thee haughty tyrants ne'er shall tame!
  All their attempts to bend thee down,
Will but arouse thy generous flame!
  But work their woe, and thy renown!
    Rule, Britannia! rule the waves!' &c.

'To thee belongs the rural reign;
  Thy cities shall with commerce shine!
All thine shall be the subject Main;
  And every shore it circles thine!
    Rule, Britannia! rule the waves!' &c.

James Thomson.

'The Muses, still with Freedom found,
  Shall to thy happy coast repair!
Blest Isle! with matchless beauty crowned;
  And manly hearts to guard the Fair!
    Rule, BRITANNIA! rule the waves!' &c.

For ever, FORTUNE! wilt thou prove
An unrelenting foe to Love!
And when we meet a mutual heart,
Come in between, and bid us part!

Bid us sigh on, from day to day;
And wish, and wish the soul away!
Till youth and genial years are flown;
And all the life of life is gone!

But busy, busy still art thou,
To bind the loveless, joyless vow!
The heart from pleasure to delude!
To join the gentle to the rude!

For once, O, FORTUNE! hear my prayer;
And I absolve thy future care!
All other blessings I resign;
Make but the dear AMANDA mine!

James Thomson.

HARD is the fate of him who loves;
   Yet dares not tell his trembling pain
But to the sympathetic groves!
   But to the lonely listening plain!

O, when She blesses next your shade,
   O, when her footsteps next are seen
In flowery tracts along the mead,
   In fresher mazes o'er the Green;

Ye gentle Spirits of the Vale!
   (To whom the tears of love are dear)
From dying lilies waft a gale,
   And sigh my sorrows in her ear!

O, tell her, what She cannot blame,
   Though fear my tongue must ever bind,
O, tell her, that my virtuous flame
   Is as her spotless soul refined!

Not her own guardian angel eyes
   With chaster tenderness his care!
Not purer her own wishes rise!
   Not holier her own sighs in prayer!

But if, at first, her virgin fear
   Should start at Love's suspected name;
With that of Friendship soothe her ear!
   True Love and Friendship are the same!

James Thomson.

O, NIGHTINGALE! best poet of the grove!
   That plaintive strain can ne'er belong to thee,
Blessed in the full possession of thy love!
   O, lend that strain, sweet nightingale! to me!

'Tis mine, alas! to mourn my wretched fate!
   I love a Maid, who all my bosom charms;
Yet lose my days, without this lovely mate!
   Inhuman Fortune keeps her from my arms!

You, happy birds! by Nature's simple laws,
   Lead your soft lives, sustained by Nature's fare!
You dwell wherever roving fancy draws;
   And Love and Song is all your pleasing care.

But we (vain slaves of Interest and Pride!)
   Dare not be blessed, lest envious tongues should blame!
And hence, in vain, I languish for my Bride!
   O, mourn with me, sweet bird! my hapless flame!

ONE day, the God of fond desire,
   On mischief bent, to DAMON said,
'Why not disclose your tender fire?
   Not own it to the lovely Maid?'

The Shepherd marked his treacherous art;
  And, softly sighing, thus replied.
''Tis true, you have subdued my heart;
  But shall not triumph o'er my pride!

'The slave, in private only bears
  Your bondage, who his love conceals;
But when his Passion he declares,
  You drag him at your chariot wheels!'

COME, gentle God of soft desire!
  Come, and possess my happy breast!
Not, Fury-like, in flames and fire;
  Or frantic Folly's wildness drest.

But come in Friendship's angel-guise;
  Yet dearer thou, than Friendship art!
More tender spirit in thy eyes!
  More sweet emotions at the heart!

O, come, with Goodness in thy Train!
  With Peace, and Pleasure void of storm!
And wouldst thou me for ever gain;
  Put on AMANDA's winning form!

James Thomson.

TO SERAPHINA.

The Wanton's charms, however bright,
Are like the false illusive light;
Whose flatt'ring unauspicious blaze,
To precipices oft betrays.
But that sweet ray your beauties dart,
Which clears the mind, and cleans the heart,
Is like the sacred Queen of Night:
Who pours a lovely gentle light
Wide o'er the dark; by wanderers blest,
Conducting them to peace and rest.

A vicious love depraves the mind!
'Tis Anguish, Guilt, and Folly joined!
But SERAPHINA's eyes dispense
A mild and gracious influence;
Such as, in visions, Angels shed
Around the heaven-illumined head.
To love thee, SERAPHINA! sure,
Is to be tender, happy, pure!
'Tis from low Passions to escape;
And woo bright Virtue's fairest shape!
'Tis ecstasy, with wisdom joined;
And Heaven infused into the mind!

Richard West.

'Thanks, Chloe! Thy coquetting art,
At length, hath healed my love-sick heart!
  At length, thy slave is free!
I feel no tyrant's proud control!
I feel no inmate in my soul
  But Peace and Liberty!

'Put on thy looks of cold disdain;
Or speak respectful! 'Tis in vain!
  Nor frowns, nor smiles can move!
Those lips no more have words to bind!
Those eyes no more have light to find
  The path that leads to Love!

'But still I hear you, smiling, say,
"'Tis sign you've flung your chains away;
  You take such pains to show them!"
Why, Chloe! there's a fond delight,
Our former dangers to recite;
  And let our neighbours know them!

Richard West.

'After the thunder of the wars;
The Vet'ran thus displays his scars,
   And tells you of his pains!
The Galley Slave, enslaved no more,
Shows you the shackles which he wore,
   And where their mark remains!

'For me, I quit a fickle Fair!
CHLOE has lost a heart sincere!
   Who first should sing *Te Deum*?
You'll never find so true a Swain!
But women full as false and vain,
   By dozens one may see them!'

DEAR GRAY! that always in my heart
Possessest far the better part,
What mean these sudden blasts that rise
And drive the Zephyrs from the skies?
O, join with mine, thy tuneful Lay,
And invocate the tardy May!

Come, fairest Nymph! resume thy reign!
Bring all the Graces in thy Train!

Richard West.

With balmy breath, and flowery tread,
Rise from thy soft ambrosial bed;
Where, in Elysian slumber bound,
Embow'ring myrtles veil thee round.

Awake, in all thy glories drest!
Recall the Zephyrs from the West!
Restore the sun! revive the skies!
At mine, and Nature's call, arise!
Great Nature's self upbraids thy stay;
And misses her accustomed May.

See! all her works demand thy aid!
The labours of POMONA fade!
A plaint is heard from ev'ry tree!
Each budding flow'ret calls for thee!
The birds forget to love and sing!
With storms alone the forests ring!

Come then, with Pleasure at thy side!
Diffuse thy vernal spirit wide!
Create, where'er thou turn'st thy eye,
Peace, Plenty, Love, and Harmony;
Till ev'ry being share its part,
And Heaven and Earth be glad at heart!

Sir Charles Hanbury Williams, K.B.

A BALLAD

IN IMITATION OF MARTIAL, LIB. VI. EP. 34., ON LADY [ELIZABETH] ILCHESTER ASKING LORD ILCHESTER, HOW MANY KISSES HE WOULD HAVE?

Written at Redlynch [Park, Somerset], in August 1740.

DEAR BETTY! come, give me sweet kisses!
   For sweeter no Girl ever gave!
But why, in the midst of our blisses,
   Do you ask me, How many I'd have?
I'm not to be stinted in pleasure,
   Then, prithee, dear BETTY! be kind!
For as I love thee beyond measure,
   To numbers I'll not be confined!

Count the bees that on Hybla are straying!
   Count the flowers that enamel the fields!
Count the flocks that on Tempe are playing;
   Or the grains that each Sicily yields!
Count how many stars are in heaven!
   Go, reckon the sands on the shore!
And when so many kisses you've given;
   I still shall be asking for more!

Sir Charles Hanbury Williams, K.B.

To a heart full of love, let me hold thee!
　A heart that, dear BETTY! is thine!
In my arms I'll for ever enfold thee;
　And curl round thy neck like a vine!
What joy can be greater than this is?
　My life on thy lips shall be spent!
But those who can number their kisses,
　Will always with few be content!

A SONG ON MISS HARRIET HANBURY,

ADDRESSED TO THE REV. MR. BIRT.

DEAR Doctor of St. Mary's,
In the Hundred of Bergavenny,
　　I've seen such a Lass,
　　With a shape and face
As never were matched by any.

Such wit, such bloom, and beauty,
Has this girl of Pontypool, Sir!
　　With eyes that would make
　　The toughest heart ache,
And the wisest man a fool, Sir!

At our Fair, t' other day, she appeared, Sir!
And the Welshmen all flocked and viewed her:
　　And all of them said,
　　'She was fit to have been made
A Wife for OWEN TUDOR!'

Sir Charles Hanbury Williams, K.B.

They would ne'er have been tired with gazing!
And so much her charms did please, Sir!
    That all of them stayed
    Till their ale grew dead,
And cold was their toasted cheese, Sir!

How happy the Lord of the Manor
That shall be of her possessed, Sir!
    For all must agree,
    Who my HARRIET shall see,
She 's a HARRIET [*heriot*] of the best, Sir!

Then, pray make a Ballad about her!
We know you have wit, if you'd show it.
    Then don't be ashamed!
    You can never be blamed;
For a Prophet is often a Poet!

'But why don't you make one yourself, then?'
I suppose I, by you shall be told, Sir!
    This beautiful piece,
    Alas! is my niece;
And, besides, she 's but five years old, Sir!

But though, my dear friend, she 's no older;
In her face, it may plainly be seen, Sir!
    That this Angel at five
    Will, if she 's alive,
Be a Goddess at fifteen, Sir!

Sir Charles Hanbury Williams, K.B.

At St. Osyth's, near the Mill,
   There dwells a lovely Lass.
O, had I her good will,
   How sweetly life would pass!

No bold intruding care,
   Our bliss should e'er annoy!
Her looks can gild despair;
   And heighten every joy!

Like Nature's rural scene,
   Her artless beauties charm!
Like them, with joy serene
   Our wishing hearts they warm!

Her wit, with sweetness crowned,
   Steals ev'ry sense away!
The list'ning Swains around
   Forget the short'ning day!

Health, Freedom, Wealth, and Ease,
   Without her tasteless are!
She gives them power to please;
   And makes them worth our care.

Is there, ye Powers! a bliss
   Reservèd for my share?
Indulgent, hear my wish;
   And grant it all in her!

Thomas Catesby Paget, Lord Paget.

THE CHARACTER OF ALMENON.

OUT OF AN OLD MANUSCRIPT.

ALMENON had a sort of merit!
Some sense, good humour, wit, and spirit;
But then, he had a strange weak side!
He hated roguery and pride;
Nor saw at Court, without a sneer,
The mummeries he met with there.
   To Senates, by his country sent,
He served them well in Parliament;
Nor would, for tawdry toys, or pelf,
Betray his trust, and sell himself.
   Sincere and friendly, not punctilious;
No Mamamouche, nor supercilious:
In conversation gay and free,
But liked not too much company.
   No toping sot, nor noted rake;
But yet would too much pleasure take:
Though he ne'er hurt estate, or fame;
Nor brought a scandal on the name.
   Good books he prized from earliest youth;
And valued men for worth and truth.

Thomas Catesby Paget, Lord Paget.

Chitchat he loved; but could not bear
Dull jokes, nor spiteful tales, to hear:
And rather chose to spend the day
Alone, in his amusing way,
Than barter time, and health, and quiet,
For idle news, and noisy riot.
  He could not fawn on fools and knaves;
Nor live with sycophants and slaves:
But still preferred the lone retreat
To being, that way, rich and great.

*Say! What became of this odd creature,
So out of fashion, out of Nature?*

Luck he had little; favour, less:
Nor did much worldly means possess;
Though born to Title and estate,
So whimsically odd his fate!
Yet he, with joy, gave all he could
To do his needy neighbours good.
To studious ease was much inclined;
And blessed with a contented mind.
Obscure, a peaceful life he led;
Nor envied those, who better sped.

Robert Dodsley.

THE PETITION.

The various Suppliants which address
   Their prayers to Heaven on bended knees,
All hope alike for happiness;
   Yet each petition disagrees!
Fancy, not Judgement, constitutes their bliss!
The wise, no doubt, will say the same of this!

'Ye Gods! if you remember right,
   Some eighteen years ago,
A Form was made divinely bright;
   And sent for us t' admire below.
I first distinguished her from all the rest;
And hope you'll therefore think my title best!

'I ask not heaps of shining gold!
   No! If the Gods vouchsafe
My longing arms may her infold;
   I'm rich, I'm rich enough!
Riches, at best, can hardly give content;
But having her, What is there I can want?

'I ask not, with a pompous Train
   Of honours, all th' World t' outbrave.
The title I would wish to gain
   Is "her most fav'rite slave!"
To bow to her, a greater bliss would be
Than Kings and Princes bowing down to me!

Robert Dodsley.

'To rule the World with power supreme,
   Let meaner souls aspire!
To gain the sov'reignty from them,
   I stoop not to desire!
Give me to reign sole Monarch in her breast;
Let petty Princes for the World contest!

'Let libertines, who take delight
   In riot and excess,
Thus waste the day, thus spend the night;
   While I, to joys sublimer press!
Clasped in her snowy arms, such bliss I'd prove
As never yet was found, or felt, in love!

'In short, I ask you, not to live
   A tedious length of days!
Old age can little pleasure give,
   When health and strength decays!
Let but what time I have, be spent with hers;
Each moment will be worth a thousand years!'

MAN's a poor deluded Bubble,
   Wand'ring in a mist of lies;
Seeing false, or seeing double,
   Who would trust to such weak eyes?
Yet presuming on his senses,
   On he goes, most wondrous wise!
Doubts of truth! believes pretences!
   Lost in error lives, and dies!

Robert Dodsley.

THE ADVICE.

    Dost thou, my friend! desire to rise
To Honour, Wealth, and Dignities?
Virtue's paths, though trod by few,
With constant steps do thou pursue!
    For as the coward soul admires
That courage which the Brave inspires;
And, his own quarrels to defend,
Gladly makes such a one his friend:
So in a World which Rogues infest,
How is an Honest Man carest!
The villains from each other fly;
And on his virtue safe rely!

Robert Dodsley.

How happy a state does the Miller possess!
Who would be no greater; nor fears to be less!
On his Mill and himself, he depends for support;
Which is better than servilely cringing at Court!

What though he all dusty and whitened does go;
The more he 's bepowdered, the more like a Beau!
A Clown in this dress may be honester far
Than a Courtier who struts in his Garter and Star!

Though his hands are so daubed they're not fit to be seen;
The hands of his betters are not very clean!
A palm more polite may as dirtily deal;
Gold, in handling, will stick to the fingers like meal!

What if, when a pudding for dinner he lacks,
He cribs, without scruple, from other men's sacks:
In this, of right noble examples he brags;
Who borrow as freely from other men's bags!

Or should he endeavour to heap an estate;
In this he would mimic the tools of the State!
Whose aim is alone their own coffers to fill;
As all his concern 's to bring grist to his mill.

He eats when he 's hungry; he drinks when he 's dry;
And down, when he 's weary, contented does lie:
Then rises up cheerful to work and to sing.
If so happy a Miller; then who'd be a King?

Anonymous.

WHY, CELIA! should you so much strive,
  Your kindling Passion to conceal?
Your lips, though they denial give;
  Yet all your actions, love reveal!

In vain you strive, in vain, alas!
  The charming Passion to disguise!
It glows, it blushes, on your face;
  And sparkles in your swimming eyes!

Your eyes, those emblems of the heart,
  Still contradict whate'er you say:
And though your lips deny the smart;
  Your eyes are more believed than they!

'TELL me, EUNESIA! prithee, tell!
(For thou, I fancy, know'st me well!)
Tell me, Why I, who was so gay
(I laughed, I revelled, all the day!),
Who life enjoyed, and feared not Fate,
Why am I altered thus of late?

Anonymous.

    Tasteless are grown my former joys!
Wit is but folly; Music, noise!
So unattentive is my mind,
In crowds a solitude I find!
While all my friends are joyous seen,
Musing I sit. 'Ha! what ails BEN?'
One cries, ''Tis pride!'; another, 'spleen!'
Reproached thus, I'll go read! But what?
SHAKESPEARE is lifeless! MILTON, flat!
    Successive pleasures thus I try,
From thought to thought for comfort fly;
But none I find! Nothing can please!
Books and acquaintance only tease!
So restless is my soul, I own
Life is itself a burthen grown!
What means all this? Where can it end?
Tell me, my Charmer and my friend!'

    'What,' said EUNESIA, 'what means this?
Are you so dull, you cannot guess?
Fly, my AMINTOR! to my arms!
(Where you've confessed a thousand charms!)
Fly to my arms! You'll quickly find
'Tis absence only stings your mind!
Fly to my arms! A kiss I'll give
That shall your gaiety revive;
And make you own, you wish to live!'

THE MUTUAL SYMPTOMS.

'Ah! who, in all those happy plains,
  With Colin may compare!
A Youth beloved of all the Swains;
  Admired by all the Fair.
I think he 's free from artful wiles:
  For oft, with tearful eye,
He fondly looks at me, and smiles.
  He does! I know not Why?

'He pressed my hand. I blushed and sighed;
  Yet hope he did not see!
And then to speak he vainly tried;
  But gently sighed, like me!
Methinks, this wary breast should know
  If Colin feigned the sigh;
Yet when he 's named, it flutters so!
  It does! I know now Why?

Say, gentle God! whose mighty laws
  Prevail o'er Nymph and Swain;
O, shew my heart the secret cause
  Of Colin's tender pain!
Say rather, why this heart *intreats*
  The cause of Colin's woe!
And why it flutters! why it beats!
  Alas! too well I know!'

The End of The Pope Anthology.

FIRST LINES AND NOTES.

Many of these Poems became immediately popular; and appeared in other contemporary editions than those here quoted, often with great variations in the texts.
All the Works herein quoted, were published in London; unless otherwise stated.
Where a text is found associated with music, (M.) is put after its date.

	PAGE
A band of Cupids, th' other day ..	137
Hon. M. MONK. *Poems, &c.*, 1716.	
A Bard, grown desirous of saving	229
ANON. In *Miscellaneous Poems*, ed. by M. CONCANEN, 1724.	
A Cobbler there was, and he lived	222
ANON. In *Musical Miscellany*, II, 1729. (M.)	
A decent mien, an elegance of dress	207
R. SAVAGE. In *Miscellaneous Poems*, ed. by him, 1726.	
A famous Assembly was	132
J. SHEFFIELD, Duke of BUCKINGHAM. *Works*, 1723.	
Ah! gaze not on those eyes!	277
C. COCKBURN. *Works*, 1751.	
'Ah! who, in all those happy	300
ANON. In a *Collection of Songs*, set by Mr. PIXELL, Birmingham [1745].	
Alexis shunned his fellow Swains	74
M. PRIOR. *Poems*, 1709.	
All in the Downs the Fleet was....	160
J. GAY. *Poems*, 1720.	
Almenon had a sort of merit......	292
T. C. PAGET, Lord PAGET. In his *Miscellanies*, 1741.	
Alone, by a lonely willow..........	273
H. CAREY. *Poems*, 3rd Ed., 1729.	
As, after noon, one summer's day	79
M. PRIOR. *Poems*, 1709.	
As Chloe on flowers reclined o'er .	253
Rev. J. HOADLY; usually called Mr. Chancellor HOADLY. In R. DODSLEY's *Collection, &c.*, V, 1758.	
A silly Shepherd wooed; but wist	122
ANON. In J. DRYDEN's *Miscellany Poems*, VI, 1716.	
At night, by moonlight, on the plain	230
E. ROOME. His alteration of R. BROME's *Jovial Crew*, 1731.	
A trifling Song you shall hear	64
G. FARQUHAR. *Beaux' Stratagem* (1707), in *Comedies*, 1728.	
At St. Osyth's, near the Mill	291
Sir C. H. WILLIAMS, K.B. *Works*, 1822.	
A wanton Bee, of ancient fame....	201
E. HOWARD, Earl of SUFFOLK. In his *Miscellanies*, 1725.	
Away! Let nought to Love........	208
ANON. In *Miscellaneous Poems*, ed. by D. LEWIS, 1726.	
A wretch, long tortured with	121
ANON. In *Poetical Miscellanies*, ed. by Sir R. STEELE, 1714.	

	PAGE
Behind her neck her comely	86
M. PRIOR. *Poems*, 1709.	
Behold, my friend! the	215
W. SOMERVILE. *Occasional Poems, &c.*, 1727.	
Belinda! see, from yonder flowers	95
ANON. In *The Spectator*, No. 473, September 2, 1712.	
Beneath a myrtle's verdant shade	68
M. PRIOR. *Poems*, 1709.	
Beneath some hoary mountain....	45
Rt. Hon. JOSEPH ADDISON. *Rosamond*, 1707.	
Blest as th' immortal Gods is he ..	105
A. PHILIPS. *The Spectator*, No. 229, Nov. 22, 1711. The text is that of *Pastorals, &c.*, 1748. From SAPPHO. For Mrs. A. BEHN's version, see Vol. VII, 162.	
But anxious cares the pensive	23
A. POPE. *Rape of the Lock*, 5th Ed., 1718.	
Cease, fair Calistris! cease........	51
M., Lady CHUDLEIGH. *Poems*, 1703.	
Cease, fond Shepherd! Cease	145
Lady M. W. MONTAGU. *Works*, 1803.	
Cease your funning!................	171
J. GAY. *The Beggar's Opera*, 1728.	
Cease your music, gentle Swains!	107
A. PHILIPS. *Pastorals, &c.*, 1748.	
Celia and I, the other day..........	82
M. PRIOR. *Poems*, 1709.	
Close by those meads for ever	16
A. POPE. *Rape of the Lock*, 1st Ed., 1714.	
Come, gentle God of soft desire! ..	283
J. THOMSON. *Poems*, 1750.	
Come, let us now resolve at last ..	131
J. SHEFFIELD, Duke of BUCKINGHAM. *Works*, 1723.	
Cupid and Fortune long agreed ..	258
ANON. In *Miscellany*, ed. by J. HUSBANDS, Oxf., 1731.	
Cupid and Venus jointly strove ..	251
W. POPPLE. In *Miscellaneous Poems*, ed. by R. SAVAGE, 1726.	
'Cupid! instruct an am'rous	54
W. WALSH. In J. DRYDEN's *Miscellany Poems*, V, 1704.	

301

First Lines and Notes.

	PAGE
Cursed be the wretch that's	272

H. CAREY. *Poems*, 3rd Ed., 1729. The last two lines are from *Musical Miscellany*, V, 1731. (M.)

Daphne, the beautiful and coy 157
W. BEDINGFIELD. In A. H. [A. HAMMOND]'s *New Miscellany*, 1720.
Daphnis stood pensive in the 164
J. GAY. *Poems*, 1720.
Dear Betty! come, give me sweet 288
Sir C. H. WILLIAMS, K.B. *Works*, 1822.
Dear Colin! prevent my warm ... 142
I. CONWAY, Countess of HERTFORD. In R. DODSLEY's *Collection, &c.*, VI, 1758.
Dear Doctor of St. Mary's 289
Sir C. H. WILLIAMS, K.B. *Works*, 1822.
Dear Gray! that always in my 286
R. WEST. In J. GRAY's *Poems*, York, 1775.
Delia! how long must I despair .. 240
G. GRANVILLE, Lord LANSDOWNE. *Works*, 1732.
Despairing, beside a clear stream.. 125
N. ROWE, P.L. *Poetical Works*, 2nd Ed., 1720.
Did ever Swain, a Nymph adore .. 242
C. HAMILTON, Lord BINNING. In *Gentleman's Magazine* for March, 1741.
'Did our sighing Lovers know 220
E. ROOME. His alteration of R. BROME's *Jovial Crew*, 1731.
Disarmed with so genteel an Air.. 109
A. FINCH, Countess of WINCHILSEA. In P. BAYLE's *Dictionary*, X, 1741.
Distracted with care 52
W. WALSH. In J. DRYDEN's *Miscellany Poems*, V, 1704.
Dost thou, my friend! desire to rise 296
R. DODSLEY. *Trifles*, 1745.

Every man take his Glass in his .. 228
ANON. In *Musical Miscellany*, III, 1730. (M.)

Fair Amoret is gone astray! 60
W. CONGREVE. *Works*, 1710.
Fair Sally loved a bonny Sailor .. 254
Rev. J. HOADLY. In *Gentleman's Magazine* for October, 1736.

302

	PAGE
Fair Venus! whose delightful	248

G. LYTTELTON, Lord LYTTELTON. In R. DODSLEY's *Collection, &c.*, II, 1748.
False though She be to me and.... 57
W. CONGREVE. *Works*, 1710.
Farewell, my Mistress! I'll be 130
ANON. In J. DRYDEN's *Miscellany Poems*, VI, 1716.
'Fire, Water, Woman, are Man's.. 75
M. PRIOR. *Poems*, 1709.
Florella! when those eyes I see .. 96
W. HARRISON. In J. NICHOL's *Select Collection, &c.*, 1782.
Fly from false Man! Dorinda, fly! 149
ANON. In G. VANBRUGHE's *Mirth and Harmony* [1720]. (M.)
'Foolish Love! be gone!' said I.. 239
G. GRANVILLE, Lord LANSDOWNE. *Works*, 1732.
For ever, Fortune! wilt thou prove 280
J. THOMSON. *Poems*, 1750.
'Frae great Apollo, Poet say 183
A. RAMSAY. *Poems*, Edin., I, 1724.
From place to place forlorn I go .. 63
Capt. Sir R. STEELE. *The Conscious Lovers*, 1723.
From the Court, to the Cottage.... 276
H. CAREY. In his *Musical Century*, 1737.
From White's and Will's 108
A. PHILIPS. In *Poetical Miscellanies*, ed. by Sir R. STEELE, 1714.

Gay Bacchus, liking Estcourt's .. 116
Archdeacon T. PARNELL, D.D. *Poems*, ed. A. POPE, 1722. The earlier text in *Poetical Miscellanies*, ed. by Sir R. STEELE, 1714, has the stanza in brackets.
'Gentle Love! this hour befriend.. 128
A. HILL. *Works*, 1753.
Gentlest air, the breath of Lovers! 94
ANON. *Poems on variety of subjects*, 1710.
Gently, my Lute! move ev'ry 214
W. SOMERVILE. *Occasional Poems, &c.*, 1727.
Give me a Lass with a lump of 181
A. RAMSAY. *Poems*, II, Edin., 1728. The text is that of the *Musical Miscellany*, VI, 1731. (M.)
God bless the King! I mean the .. 103
J. BYROM, F.R.S. *Miscellaneous Poems*, Manchester, 1773.
God save great George our King!.. 274
H. CAREY.
God save our Lord the King 275
H. CAREY.
Good Madam! when Ladies are .. 143
Lady M. W. MONTAGU. In R. DODSLEY's *Collection, &c.*, VI, 1758.

First Lines and Notes.

	PAGE
'Go, rose, my Chloe's bosom grace!	159
J. GAY. *Fables*, 1727.	
'Grant me, gentle Love,' said I	59
W. CONGREVE. *Works*, 1710.	
Happy the man! whose wish and ..	2
A. POPE. *Odes*, in *Works*, 1736.	
Hard is the fate of him who loves	281
J. THOMSON. *Poems*, 1750.	
Here, Cupid puffed, and strung his	200
E. HOWARD, Earl of SUFFOLK. In his *Miscellanies*, 1725.	
Here lies the Lyric, who, with Tale	209
ANON. In *Miscellaneous Poems*, ed. by D. LEWIS, 1726.	
Here's a Health to the Queen, and	37
ANON. As printed by Mr. W. CHAPPELL in his *Popular Music of the Olden Time*. (M.)	
How blyth, ilk morn, was I to see ..	194
S. R. In A. RAMSAY's *Tea Table Miscellany*, Edin., 1724.	
How brimful of Nothing's the life	265
Rev. J. MILLER. *Coffee House*, 1737.	
How firmly fixed, I thought my	226
J. THURSTON. *Poems*, 1729.	
How happy a state does the Miller	297
R. DODSLEY. *The King and the Miller of Mansfield*, in *Trifles*, 1745.	
How happy could I be with either	170
J. GAY. *The Beggar's Opera*, 1728.	
'How sweetly smells the simmer ..	182
A. RAMSAY. *Poems* Edin., II, 1728.	
I am, in truth, a Country Youth ..	269
H. CAREY. In *British Musical Miscellany*, IV [August, 1735]. (M.)	
Ianthe the lovely, the joy of her ..	55
J. GLANVILL. *Poems*, 1725. This is the answering political Poem to DRYDEN's in Vol. VII, 20. IANTHE is Queen ANNE; and IPHIS, Prince GEORGE, her husband.	
If those who live in Shepherd's	278
J. THOMSON and D. MALLET. *Alfred*, a Masque, 1740. It is thought that its Songs are by THOMSON.	
'If thou hadst liberty to choose ..	233
ANON. In *Miscellany*, ed. by J. HUSBANDS, Oxf., 1731.	
If 'tis joy to wound a Lover........	45
Rt. Hon. JOSEPH ADDISON. *Rosamond*, 1707.	
If Wine and Music have the power	80
M. PRIOR. *Poems*, 1709.	
I know the thing that's most......	1
A. POPE. *Works*, 1751.	

	PAGE
'I'll tell her, the next time!' said I	239
G. GRANVILLE, Lord LANSDOWNE. *Works*, 1732.	
I looked, and I sighed, and I wished	58
W. CONGREVE. *Old Batchelor*, in *Works*, 1710.	
I love! but She alone shall know ..	67
P. A. MOTTEUX. In J. O. [J. OLDMIXON]'s *Muses' Mercury* for March, 1707.	
In Beauty, or Wit	150
A. POPE. In A. H. [A. HAMMOND]'s *New Miscellany*, 1720.	
In Church, the 'Prayer Book' and	149
ANON. In *Poetical Miscellanies*, ed. by Sir R. STEELE, 1714.	
In good King Charles's golden	147
ANON. In *British Musical Miscellany*, I [January, 1734]. (M.)	
In Heaven, one holiday, you read .	71
M. PRIOR. *Poems*, 1709.	
In London stands a famous Pile ..	175
E. WARD. *Delights of the Bottle*, [Sept.] 1720.	
In such a night, when every louder	112
A. FINCH, Countess of WINCHILSEA. *Miscellany Poems*, 1713.	
In two large columns on thy	152
Lady M. W. MONTAGU and J. HERVEY, Lord HERVEY. The original folio issue of these *Verses, &c.* [1733].	
In vain, dear Cloe! you suggest ..	236
Rt. Hon. Sir W. YONGE, Bart. In *Musical Miscellany*, III, 1730. (M.)	
In vain, you boast poetic names ..	109
A. POPE. In P. BAYLE's *Dictionary*, X, 1741.	
In vain, you tell your parting	70
M. PRIOR. *Poems*, 1709.	
I said to my heart, between sleeping	225
C. MORDAUNT, Earl of PETERBOROUGH. In SWIFT and POPE's *Miscellanies*, 1727.	
I slyly stole this secret Charm	227
J. THURSTON. *Poems*, 1729.	
'It always has been thought	89
M. PRIOR. *The Conversation*. The original folio issue of 1720.	
It must be so! Plato, thou reason'st	48
Rt. Hon. J. ADDISON. *Cato*, 1713.	
I took the paper in my trembling ..	129
A. HILL. *Works*, 1753.	
Let not Love on me bestow........	62
Capt. Sir R. STEELE. *The Funeral*, 1702.	
Let them censure! what care I? ..	81
M. PRIOR. *Poems*, 1709.	
Life is a jest; and all things show	166
J. GAY. *Poems*, 1720.	

First Lines and Notes.

	PAGE
Lords, Knights, and Squires, the ..	76
M. PRIOR. In J. DRYDEN's *Miscellany Poems*, V, 1704.	
Love and Folly were at play	66
P. A. MOTTEUX. In J. O. [J. OLDMIXON]'s *Muses' Mercury* for April, 1707.	
Love's an idle childish Passion ..	232
H. BAKER, F.R.S. In *British Musical Miscellany*, I [April, 1734]. (M.)	
Love is a scion cropped from......	61
T. ELLWOOD. In his *Collection of Poems* [1730].	
Love, wearied with his roving	97
ANON In *Oxford and Cambridge Miscellany Poems*, ed. by E. FENTON, [1709]. This Poem is on the same subject as PRIOR's at p. 86, published in the same year.	

Man's a poor deluded Bubble	295
R. DODSLEY. *Trifles*, 1745.	
Me Cupid made a happy slave	63
Capt. Sir R. STEELE. In J. O. [J. OLDMIXON]'s *Muses' Mercury* for February, 1707.	
My days have been so wondrous	114
Archdeacon T. PARNELL, D.D. In *Poetical Miscellanies*, ed. by Sir R. STEELE, 1714.	
My time, O, ye Muses! was happily	100
J. BYROM, F.R.S. *The Spectator*, No. 603, October 6, 1714. The text is from *Miscellaneous Poems*, Manchester, 1773.	

Not with more glories in th'........	10
A. POPE. *Rape of the Lock*, 1st Ed., 1714.	
No warning of th' approaching	238
G. GRANVILLE, Lord LANSDOWNE. *Works* 1732.	

Of all the Girls that are so smart..	266
H. CAREY. *Poems*, 3rd Ed., 1729.	
Of all the torments, all the cares..	52
W. WALSH. In J. DRYDEN's *Miscellany Poems*, V, 1704.	
Of Leinster, famed for Maidens ..	172
T. TICKELL. In R. DODSLEY's *Collection, &c.*, I, 1748.	
O, forbear to bid me slight her! ..	128
A. HILL. *Works*, 1753.	

	PAGE
Oft hast thou told me, Dick! in ..	186
N. AMHURST. *Poems*, 1723.	
O, grant that Marshal Wade	275
ANON.	
O, I'll have a husband! aye	271
H. CAREY. In Sir J. VANBRUGH and C. CIBBER's *Provoked Husband*, 2nd Ed., 1729.	
One day, the God of fond desire ..	282
J. THOMSON. *Poems*, 1750.	
O, nightingale! best poet of the....	282
J. THOMSON. *Poems*, 1750.	
On Thames's bank, a gentle Youth	240
G. LYTTELTON, Lord LYTTELTON. In R. DODSLEY's *Collection, &c.*, II, 1748.	
O, ruddier than the cherry!........	159
J. GAY. *Acis and Galatea*, 1732.	
O, say, What is that thing called ..	257
C. CIBBER, P.L. In *British Musical Miscellany*, I [March, 1734]. (M.)	
O, the pleasing, pleasing anguish..	45
Rt. Hon. JOSEPH ADDISON. *Rosamond*, 1707.	
'O, Venus! Beauty of the skies!..	104
A. PHILIPS. *The Spectator*, No. 223, Nov. 15, 1711. The text is that of *Pastorals, &c.*, 1748. From SAPPHO.	

Persuade me not, there is a grace..	111
A. FINCH, Countess of WINCHILSEA. *Miscellany Poems*, 1713.	
Phillis is lively, brisk, and gay....	200
E. HOWARD, Earl of SUFFOLK. In his *Miscellanies*, 1725.	
Polly! from me, though now a	206
R. SAVAGE. *Works*, 1775.	
Pope has the talent well to speak..	211
Dean J. SWIFT. *Poetical Works*, 1736.	
Prithee, tell me, What a Beau is ?..	98
ANON. *Poems, &c.*, published by J. PEMBERTON, 1714.	

Reading ends in melancholy!	85
M. PRIOR. *Miscellaneous Works*, 1740.	

Say, Myra! why is gentle Love ..	246
G. LYTTELTON, Lord LYTTELTON. In R. DODSLEY's *Collection, &c.*, II, 1748.	

First Lines and Notes.

	PAGE
Says my uncle, 'I pray you	167
J. GAY. In SWIFT and POPE'S *Miscellanies*, 1727.	
See! see, she wakes! Sabina......	57
W. CONGREVE. *Works*, 1710.	
She said. The pitying audience ..	30
A. POPE. *Rape of the Lock*, 5th Ed., 1718.	
She was not coy!	218
E. ROOME. His alteration of R. BROME's *Jovial Crew*, 1731.	
Soft kisses may be innocent	277
C. COCKBURN. *Works*, 1751.	
Stella and Flavia, ev'ry hour......	221
M. BARBER. *Poems*, 1734.	
Sure, Cloe just, and Cloe fair......	78
M. PRIOR. *Poems*, Dublin, 1723.	
Sweet are the charms of her I love	140
B. BOOTH. In *Musical Miscellany*, II, 1729. (M.)	
'Tell me, Eunesia! prithee, tell!..	298
ANON. In *Miscellaneous Poems*, ed. by J. RALPH, 1729.	
Thanks, Chloe! Thy coquetting..	285
R. WEST. In A. DALRYMPLE's *Collection, &c.*, 1796.	
The dusky night rides down the ..	261
H. FIELDING. *Don Quixote in England*, 1734.	
'The heavy hours are almost past	245
G. LYTTELTON, Lord LYTTELTON. In R. DODSLEY's *Collection, &c.*, II, 1748.	
The Lass that would know how ..	204
M. CONCANEN. In *Musical Miscellany*, I, 1729. (M.)	
The merchant, to secure his	80
M. PRIOR. *Poems*, 1709.	
The mind of a woman can never ..	219
E. ROOME. His alteration of R. BROME's *Jovial Crew*, 1731.	
The minutes, the hours, the days..	252
Rev. J. HOADLY. In R. DODSLEY's *Collection, &c.*, III, 1748.	
The Play of Love is now begun ..	264
R. LEVERIDGE. In *Musical Miscellany*, II, 1729. (M.)	
The pride of ev'ry grove I chose ..	86
M. PRIOR. *Poems*, Dublin, 1723.	
There was an a May, and she lo'ed	202
Lady G. BAILLIE. In W. THOMSON's *Orpheus Caledonius* [1725]. (M.)	
There was an old fellow at	219
E. ROOME. His alteration of R. BROME's *Jovial Crew*, 1731.	
These, equal syllables alone	3
A. POPE. *Essay on Criticism*, 1711. The lines within brackets are from the Dublin edition of 1717.	

	PAGE
'The snows are melted, and the ..	138
L. WELSTED. *Epistles, Odes, &c.*, 1724.	
The various Suppliants which	294
R. DODSLEY. *Trifles*, 1745.	
The Wanton's charms, however ..	284
J. THOMSON. *Poems*, 1750.	
Though I never got possession ..	145
LADY M. W. MONTAGU. *Works*, 1803.	
Though women, 'tis true, are but..	218
E. ROOME. His alteration of R. BROME's *Jovial Crew*, 1731.	
Thou watchful Taper, by whose ..	56
W. CONGREVE. *Works*, 1710.	
Thus Kitty, beautiful and young ..	84
M. PRIOR. *Poems*, Dublin, 1723.	
Thus to a ripe, consenting Maid ..	56
W. CONGREVE. *Old Batchelor*, in *Works*, 1710.	
Thyrsis, a young and am'rous	119
Archdeacon T. PARNELL, D.D. *Poems*, ed. A. POPE, 1722.	
To ease my troubled mind of	247
G. LYTTELTON, Lord LYTTELTON. In R. DODSLEY's *Collection, &c.*, II, 1748.	
To him who in an hour must die ..	247
G. LYTTELTON, Lord LYTTELTON. In R. DODSLEY's *Collection, &c.*, II, 1748.	
To keep thy saul frae puny strife..	185
A. RAMSAY. *Poems*, Edin., I, 1724.	
To stifle Passion is no easy thing!	120
Archdeacon T. PARNELL, D.D. In J. NICHOL.'s *Select Collection, &c.*, III, 1780.	
To wake the soul, by tender	46
A. POPE. In Rt. Hon. J. ADDISON's *Cato*, 1713.	
'Twas when the seas were roaring	162
J. GAY. *The What d' ye call it* (1715), in *Poems*, 1720.	
Unless with my Amanda blest	278
J. THOMSON. *Poems*, 1750.	
Vital spark of heav'nly flame	36
A. POPE. *Odes*, in *Works*, 1736.	
Warned, and made wise by others'	238
G. GRANVILLE, Lord LANSDOWNE. *Works*, 1732.	
Well! if ever I saw such another..	212
Dean J. SWIFT. *Poetical Works*, 1736.	

First Lines and Notes.

	PAGE
What dire offence, from am'rous..	4
A. POPE. The first Three Cantos of *The Rape of the Lock* are from the 1st Ed. of 1714; the last Two, from the 5th Ed. of 1718.	
What man, in his wits, had not....	199
Rev. S. WESLEY. *Miscellaneous Poems*, ed. by D. LEWIS, 1726.	
What Nymph should I admire, or..	78
M. PRIOR. *Poems*, Dublin, 1723.	
What! put off with one denial!....	93
J. PHILIPS. *Cider, &c.*, 1708.	
What though I am a London......	223
ANON. In *British Musical Miscellany* [March, 1734]. (M.)	
What though they call me Country	270
H. CAREY. In Sir J. VANBRUGH and C. CIBBER's *Provoked Husband*, 2nd Ed., 1729.	
What Woman could do, I have ..	256
C. CIBBER, P.L. *Love in a Riddle*, 1719.	
When all was wrapped in dark ..	178
ANON. [? Edin., ? 1723.] D. MALLET touched up this 'old Ballad'; and passed it off as his own.	
When Britain first, at Heaven's ..	279
J. THOMSON and D. MALLET. *Alfred*, a Masque. It is thought that its Songs are by THOMSON.	
When Daphne first her Shepherd..	50
M., Lady CHUDLEIGH. *Poems*, 1703.	
When Delia on the plain appears..	244
G. LYTTELTON, Lord LYTTELTON. In R. DODSLEY's *Collection, &c.*, II, 1748.	
When I think on your truth; I....	250
G. LYTTELTON, Lord LYTTELTON. In R. DODSLEY's *Collection, &c.*, II, 1748.	
When mighty Roast Beef was the .	262
H. FIELDING. *Don Quixote in England*, 1734.—R. LEVERIDGE. In *British Musical Miscellany*, III [May, 1735]. (M.)	
'When Slaves their liberty require	54
W. WALSH. In *The Grove*, 1721.	
'When thy beauty appears	115
Archdeacon T. PARNELL, D.D. *Poems*, ed. by A. POPE, 1722.	
When you censure the Age........	171
J. GAY. *The Beggar's Opera*, 1728.	
While at my house in Fleet street	124
N. ROWE, P.L. *Poetical Works*, 2nd Ed., 1720.	
While Butler, needy wretch! was	209
ANON. In *Miscellaneous Poems*, ed. by D. LEWIS, 1726.	
While from our looks, fair Nymph!	77
M. PRIOR. *Poems*, 1709.	
While gentle Parthenissa walks ..	62
Capt. Sir R. STEELE. *Tender Husband*, 1717.	

	PAGE
While you, my Lord! the rural....	38
Rt. Hon. J. ADDISON. In J. DRYDEN's *Miscellany Poems*, V, 1704.	
Why are those charms by frowns	205
M. CONCANEN. In *Miscellaneous Poems*, ed. by R. SAVAGE, 1726.	
Why, Celia! should you so much	298
ANON. In *Miscellaneous Poems*, ed. by J. RALPH, 1729.	
Why, Damon! why, why, why so	50
M., Lady CHUDLEIGH. *Poems*, 1703.	
Why, lovely Charmer! tell me	62
Capt. Sir R. STEELE. *Tender Husband*, 1717.	
Why should a heart so tender	241
G. GRANVILLE, Lord LANSDOWNE. *Works*, 1732.	
Why should those eyes, Florella!	251
W. POPPLE. In *Miscellaneous Poems*, ed. by R. SAVAGE, 1726.	
Why we love, and why we hate ..	106
A. PHILIPS. *Pastorals, &c.*, 1744.	
Why will Delia thus retire	144
Lady M. W. MONTAGU. In R. DODSLEY's *Collection, &c.*, I, 1755.	
With an honest old friend, and....	268
H. CAREY. *Poems*, 3rd Ed., 1729.	
With downcast eyes and folded ..	231
H. BAKER, F.R.S. In *Musical Miscellany*, III, 1730. (M.)	
With my frailty, don't upbraid me!	58
W. CONGREVE. *Semele*, an Opera, in *Works*, 1710.	
'Woman! thoughtless, giddy......	230
H. BAKER, F.R.S. In *Musical Miscellany*, IV, 1730. (M.)	
Ye Poets ragged and forlorn	210
Dean J. SWIFT. *Poetical Works*, 1736.	
'Ye Shepherds and Nymphs, that	198
W. HAMILTON, of Bangour. *Poems*, 1760.	
'Ye Shepherds of this pleasant....	196
W. HAMILTON, of Bangour. *Poems*, 1760.	
You ask, my friend! How I can ..	136
Rev. L. EUSDEN, P.L. In *Poetical Miscellanies*, ed. by Sir R. STEELE, 1714.	
You little know the heart, that you	146
Lady M. W. MONTAGU. *Works*, 1803.	
'Young Strephon, by his folded ..	156
W. BEDINGFIELD. In A. H. [A. HAMMOND]'s *New Miscellany*, 1720.	
Youth's the season made for joys!	170
J. GAY. *The Beggar's Opera*, 1728.	

GLOSSARY AND INDEX.

A', 183, 194, all.
Abigails (M. Prior), 84, ladies' maids.
Aboon, 184, above.
The Act Tune, 264, the Overture.
Addison, Rt. Hon. J., 38-45, 48, 49, 134.
Affectation (A. Pope), 24.
Africa, 19, 161.
Agamemnon, 33.
Ain, 182, own.
Air, 14, 62, 63, manner, bearing, appearance.
Ajax (A. Pope), 3.
Hoary Albula, 39, a stream flowing from the sulphureous Lake Albunea into the Anio, and thence into the Tiber. The latter also was anciently called Albula.
Alcander (W. Walsh), 54.
Alexandrine, 3, a line of verse of twelve syllables.
Alexis (M. Prior), 74, 75.
Almenon (T. C. Paget, Lord Paget), 292, 293.
Amanda (J. Thomson), 278, 283.
Amaryllis (J. Gay), 169.
Amhurst, N., 186-193.
Amintor (Anon.), 298, 299.
Amintor (W. Popple), 251.
Amintor (L. Welsted), 138, 139.
Amoret (W. Congreve), 60.
Amoret (J. Thurston), 227.
An Amphitheatre, 41, the Coliseum at Rome.
Amynta (W. Congreve), 59.
Amynta (W. Somervile), 215.
An, 202, once.
Animated rocks to live, 43, sculpture.
Anna, 30.
Great Anna! 16, Queen Anne.
Anne, Queen, 16, 148.
Appose, 202, suppose.
Arabia, 9.
Ardelia [= the poetical name of A. Finch, Countess of Winchelsea], 109.
Ariel, a Sylph, see Machines, 5-8, 12-15, 17, 21, 23.

Ariosto, 34.
Atalantis, 22, a satirical Romance by Mrs. M. Manley.
Atterbury, Bishop of Rochester; F., 134.
Asia, 19.
Greater Assembly, 134, the House of Commons.
Ay (*Scotch*), 185, ever.

Looking babies, 99, the small image of oneself, reflected in the pupil of another's eye.
Save his bacon, 91, to save himself from harm.
Baillie, Lady G., 202, 203.
Baith, 183, 202, both.
Baja [= Baia?], 40.
Baker, F.R.S.; H., 230-232.
Bangs me, 266, beats me.
Bannock, 184, bread, made in a round and flat shape.
Barber, M., 221.
The Baron [= Lord Petre], a little man. 5, (A. Pope), 4, 11, 18, 19, 20-22, 28, 30, 33, 34.
Bartlemew Fair, 132, held in Smithfield on St. Bartholomew's Day, August 24.
Beau (Anon.), 98, 99.
Bedingfield, W., 156-158.
Belinda (Anon.), 95.
Belinda (Anon.), 149.
Belinda [= Miss A. Fermor] (A. Pope), 4-35.
Belinda (J. Thurston), 226.
Belvidera (J. Thurston), 227.
On the bent, 184, the grass.
Berenice, 35.
Bergavenny, 289, Abergavenny, Monmouthshire.
Berries crackle, 20, the coffee berries, as they were roasted.
Betty [= Belinda's lady's-maid] (A. Pope), 9.
Betty [= Lady E. Ilchester], 288, 289.
Bevil (H. Baker, F.R.S.), 230.
Corn bing, 203, a place for storing corn.
Birt, Rev. —, 289, 290.
Birth-night Beau, 5, once elegantly dressed for the Court Ball given on a royal Birthday.

Exploded Bite, 272, a hoax, a swindle.
A Black Coat, 65, the Clergy.
A blackguard boy, 72, a boy carrying a link, or torch.
Blackmore, Sir R., 132.
Pushing Blades, 177, free and easy fellows, gallants.
Blate, 183, bashful, diffident.
The Blind Boy (C. Cibber, P.L.), 257.
A purer blush, 9, by the use of rouge.
Blyth, 194, blithe.
Bohea, 29, a kind of tea.
Boileau-Despreaux, N., 4.
To boot, 65, into the bargain.
Booth, B., 140, 141.
Painted Bow, 13, the rainbow.
Thou bows, 183, bowest.
Bows his eye, 203, shuts it.
Bow street, London, 125.
The Box, 6, at the theatre.
The Boyne, 40, in Ireland.
Bra, 202, brave, fine.
Braes, 184, banks.
Braided colours gay, 139, embroidered.
Bray, 147-149, in Berkshire.
Breathing rocks, 41, sculptures.
Brillante, a Sylph (A. Pope), 14.
Brimmers, 116, cups full to the brim.
Britain, 40, 44, 279.
Britannia, 43, 109, 279.
Britons, 272.
Brown, Sir G. [= Sir Plume] (A. Pope), 27, 28, 32.
A brushing fox, 261, a fox having a bushy tail, or brush.
A Bubble, 73, 295, a dupe, a gull.
Bubbles, 176, mad speculations.
Budgell, E., 134.
Burn, 183, stream.
Busk, 12, a strong piece of wood or whalebone in front of a corset, to stiffen it.
Butler, S., 208.
Byrom, F.R.S.; J., 100-103.

Glossary and Index.

Cæsar, C. J., 47, 49.
Cain, 155.
Calistris (M., Lady Chudleigh), 51.
Camilla (A. Pope), 3.
Camilla, 32, an Opera.
Carey, H., 266-276.
Carries me to Church, 267, compels me to go with him.
Carse o' Gowrie, 183, on the river Tay, in Scotland.
Caryl, J. E., 4.
I turned the cat in pan, 148, to make a right-about turn, to change sides.
Cato, *Uticensis*; C. P., 46-49.
Celia (Anon.), 298.
Celia (H. Baker, F.R.S.), 230.
Celia (H. Carey), 273.
Celia (M. Prior), 82, 83.
A Chair, 6, a Sedan Chair carried by two Pages.
Charles II, King, 147.
Chear'd, 194, cheered.
China's earth, 20, china coffee-cups.
Chit, 200, child.
Chloe (H. Baker, F.R.S.), 232.
Chloe (J. Gay), 159, 164-166.
Chloe (Rev. J. Hoadly), 252, 253.
Chloe (J. Thurston), 226, 227.
Chloe (R. West), 285, 286.
Chloe (Rt. Hon. Sir W. Yonge, Bart.), 236, 237.
Chloris (Rev. L. Eusden, P.L.), 136.
Chloris (Archdeacon T. Parnell, D.D.), 120.
Christy (A. Ramsay), 182, 183.
Chudleigh; M., Lady, 50, 51.
Cibber, P.L.; C., 132, 256, 257.
Cicero, M. T., 92.
Circled Green, 5, a fairy ring.
Hyde Park Circus, 37—see Ring.
Cit, 204, a citizen of London.
Clara (M. Prior), 75.
Clarissa (A. Pope), 4, 21, 30, 31, 32.
Clarke, D.D.; Rev. S., 90.
Smooth Clitumnus, 39, a branch of the Topino.
Cloe (Hon. M. Monk), 137.
Cloe [= H. Howard, Countess of Suffolk] (C. Mordaunt, Earl of Peterborough), 225. See also p. 1.
Cloe (M. Prior), 68-70, 73, 78, 79, 80, 81, 86-88.
Clorinda (M. Prior), 74, 75.
Clown, 126, 204, 291, a rustic.
Coach and Six, 22, horses.

Cob, 125, a nickname of J. Tonson.
Cockburn, C., 277.
Codille, 19, when the Challenger at Ombre loses the game.
Cœlia (W. Congreve), 58, 59.
Cœlia (C. Mordaunt, Earl of Peterborough), 225.
Cœlia (Archdeacon T. Parnell, D.D.), 119.
Cog, 168, cheat.
Colin (Anon.), 300.
Colin [the poetical name of J. Byrom, F.R.S.], 100-103.
Colin [? = Lord W. Hamilton] (? I. Conway, Countess of Hertford), 142.
Colin (Rev. J. Hoadly), 253.
Colin [= the poetical name of N. Rowe, P.L.], 125-127.
Colin (T. Tickell), 172-174.
Come-rogues, 213, fellow rogues.
Coming, 271, eager, forward, pushing.
Concanen, M., 204, 205.
Was ever concerned, 213, intoxicated, worse for liquor.
The nice conduct of a clouded cane, 28, the elegant handling of a Malacca cane.
Congreve, W., 56-60, 124, 125, 133.
Conway, Countess of Hertford; I., 142.
Cowdenknows, 194, at Earlston, Berwickshire.
Crispissa, a Sylph (A. Pope), 14.
Cryes, 202, cries.
Curll, the Publisher; E., 132, 210.
Cynthia (Rev. L. Eusden, P.L.), 136.
Cynthia (A. Pope), 23.

Daffs, 201, daffodils.
Damon (H. Baker, F.R.S.), 232.
Damon (H. Carey), 273.
Damon (M., Lady Chudleigh), 50, 51.
Damon (Lady M. W. Montagu), 144, 145.
Damon (A. Pope), 8.
Damon (M. Prior), 86-92.
Damon (J. Thomson), 282, 283.
Damon (W. Walsh), 52, 53.
Danæ, 71.
The Dane, 44, Denmark.
The Danube, 40.
Daphne, 157, 158.

Daphne (M., Lady Chudleigh), 50, 51.
Daphnis (J. Gay), 164-166.
Dapperwit (A. Pope), 32.
Dapperwit (M. Concanen), 204.
Date, 22, limit, termination.
Dawted, 184, favoured.
Dead men, 37, empty bottles.
Declaration for Liberty of Conscience, issued by James II in 1687, and again in 1688, 147.
Delany, D.D.; P., 229.
Delavall, Admiral, 125.
Delia (W. Congreve), 56, 57.
Delia (Rev. L. Eusden, P.L.), 136.
Delia (J. Gay), 166.
Delia (G. Granville, Lord Lansdowne), 240, 241.
Delia [= Miss Greville, afterwards Mrs. Boughton] (G. Lyttelton, Lord Lyttelton), 244-246.
Delia [= Lady Irwin] (Lady M. W. Montagu), 144, 145.
Delia (A. Philips), 107, 108.
Delia (J. Thurston), 227.
Delville, 229, near Dublin.
Denham, Sir J., 3.
Dennis, J., 133.
Dick (N. Amhurst), 186-193.
Dido, 30.
Discharge your quarters, 99, pay your rent.
Ran a new division, 91, spoke upon another subject.
He do, 202, to do.
Dodsley, R., 294-297.
Dollor, 202, dolour.
Dorinda (Anon.), 148.
Doughtna, 183, could not.
A' he dow do, 202, does do.
Downright Dunstable was I! 91, I used plain straightforward speech.
The Downs, 160, at Deal.
Drap, 182, drop.
Thro' the drawf, 203, on draught.
Drawing Room, 169, the royal receptions for Ladies.
Drolled, 117, jested, made fun of.
The Drops, 14, earrings.
Drusilla (E. Howard, Earl of Suffolk), 200.
D'Urfey, T., 132, 209.
Dwalm, 202, swoon.
D'ye, 92, do ye.
Dye, 202, die.

Edie [= Edward], 182, 183.
Een, 182, eyes.

Glossary and Index.

E'er, 5, &c., ever.
Eliza (Anon.), 235.
Elizabeth, Queen, 263.
Ellwood, T., 61.
Elves, 5, 13, fairies.
Eridanus [= the Po], 39.
Estcourt, R., 116. The scene of this Song is laid in the *Bumper* Tavern, in James Street, Covent Garden, London; and in 1712.
Euphelia (M. Prior), 80.
Eusden, P.L.; Rev. L., 135, 136.
Eve, 154.
Evening Post, 90, a London newspaper.
Ev'n, 4, 5, &c., even.
Ev'ry, 13, 60, &c., every.
Ews, 134, ewes.
Exchange Alley, London, 175.
Expletives, 3, empty words expanding sentences without adding to the sense.
Eunesia (Anon.), 298, 299.

Faithfu', 195, faithful.
Farquhar, G., 64, 65.
Faustina, 224.
Fenton, E., 134.
Fermor, Miss A., 4-35.
Fielding, H., 261, 262.
Fields of Death, 43, the battle-fields.
Finch, Countess of Winchilsea; A., 4, 109-113.
Project of Fish, 133, Steele's scheme for bringing fish alive to London in tanks on board fishing-boats.
Flatman, T., 36.
Flavia (M. Barber), 221.
Flavia (A. Pope), 12.
Fleet street, London, 124.
Flora (W. Bedingfield), 156, 157.
Florella (W. Harrison), 96.
Florella (W. Popple), 251.
Florinda (H. Baker, F.R.S.), 231.
Florio (A. Pope), 8.
On a foot, 65, on the same level.
Sir Fopling (A. Pope), 32.
Fortescue, afterwards Lady Lansdowne; L., 247-250.
Frae, 183-185, from.
France, 262.
Furbelow, 14, a flounce.

Gaes drooping, 203, goes about dejected, pining away.

Galileo, 35.
Gang, 181, go.
Ganymede, 71-73.
Garters, Stars, 7, 124, 175, 297, the insignia of the Orders of the Garter, the Bath, &c.
Gang any gate it will hing, 203, go any way it will hang.
The Gaul, 44, France.
Gay, J., 134, 159-171.
Gentily, 184, gently.
George I, King, 148, 149.
George II, King, 274, 275.
Gildon, C., 133.
Glanvill, J., 55.
Glass, 116, 118, 273, &c., a drinking glass.
Glass, 9, 83 144, &c., a looking-glass.
Glut, 205, satisfy.
Gold Keys in Waiting, 64, the Lord Chamberlain, &c.
Gnomes, see Machines, 6, 7, 23-26, 28, 32, 33.
Grain'd, 202, groaned.
The Grampians, 183.
Granville, Lord Lansdowne; G., 133, 238-241.
Gray, T., 286, 287.
Grub street, London. 210.

Cantily had up my crest, 185, jauntily, cheerfully hold up my head.
Hadrian, the Emperor, 36.
Hae, 183, have.
Hamilton, Lord Binning; C., 242, 243.
Hamilton, W., 196-198.
Hampton Court Palace, 16, 19, 27, 29.
Hanbury, Miss H., 289, 290.
Harrison, W., 96.
Were ne my heart's light, I wad dye! 202, 203, Were it not that my heart is brave, I would die!
The Hebrus, 110, a river in Thrace.
He'd, 222, he would.
Heeze thee, 185, raise thyself.
Heir, 99, heiress.
He'll, 51, he will.
Heroi-comical Poem, 4, mock-heroic.
Hervey, Lord Hervey; J., 152-155.
Hill, A., 128, 129.
Hoadly [usually called Mr. Chancellor Hoadly], Rev. J., 252-255.
Hogan and Nog, 169, probably Brewers about 1727.
Homer, 25, 28, 32, 33, 117.
My Honey! 267, sweet one!
Horace, 2, 152, 183.

Howard, Countess of Suffolk; H., 1, 225.
Howard, Earl of Suffolk; E., 200, 201.
Howard, Mrs.—see Howard, Countess of Suffolk; H.
Hughes, J., 134.
To hund the Tykes, 203, hound the dogs.
Hybla, 201.

Ianthe [= Queen Anne] (J. Glanvill), 55.
I'd, 268, 270, 271, &c., I would.
Ilchester, Lady E., 288, 289.
Ilchester; S., Lord, 288, 289.
Ilk, 184, 194, each.
I'll, 52, 57, 67, &c., I will.
Ill Nature (A. Pope), 24.
I'm, 57, I am.
A heavenly image, 9, that of Belinda herself.
India, 9, 161.
Iphis [= George of Denmark, Prince Consort of Queen Anne] (J. Glanvill), 55.
Lady Irwin, 144.
Italy, 38-44, 262.
Ixion, 15.

James II, King, 147.
Altars of Japan, 20, Japanese lacquered ware.
Lady Jenny (M. Prior), 84, 85.
Johnny (Lady G. Baillie), 202.
Jointured Widows, 181, having a settled separate estate.
Joliffe, J., 207.
Julia (M. Concanen), 205.

Kitchen 't, 184, sauce it.
Kitty [= Lady Katharine Hyde, afterwards Duchess of Queensberry] (M. Prior), 84, 85.

Lab'ring, 52, labouring.
Lang kail, 184, a kind of cabbage.
Latmus' peak, 86.
Leinster, Ireland, 172.
Lettle, 195, little.
Leveridge, R., 262-264.
Liffey's limpid stream, 172.
The likes of me, 202, such as me.
Lisetta (M. Prior), 78, 79.
Lockit (J. Gay), 171.
Lo'ed, 202, loved.
London, 110, 175-177.
Long Heads versus Headlongs, 175.

Glossary and Index.

Love, the affection between individuals of the opposite sexes that are capable of intermarriage.
In love.
My Love, the Lady, or Gentleman, I love.
My love, the love I have for that person.
Love-lorn, 172, forsaken, abandoned by one's Love.
Lover, a man who loves a woman. Also called, Servant, True Love.
Loww˙rds, 3, monosyllables, as in this very line.
Lu [= loo], 18, a game at cards.
Lucy [= L. Fortescue, afterwards Lady Lyttelton] (G. Lyttelton, Lord Lyttelton), 247-250.
Lucy (T. Tickell), 172-174.
Lump of land, 181, landed property.
Ly, 195, lie.
Lyttelton, Lord Lyttelton; G., 244-250.

Captain Macheath (J. Gay), 170.
Angels in Machines, 25, *ex machinâ*, the intervention of Supernatural Powers in human affairs, as Gods, Goddesses, &c.; and thence, the use of the supernatural element in Poetry.
Main, 8, 10, 70, &c., the main ocean.
Throw a Main, 71, 72, a throw of dice in gambling.
Main'd, 202, moaned.
Mair, 185, more.
Maist, 183, most.
The Mall, London, 35, 190.
[? Mallet, D., 278, 279.]
Mamamouche, 292.
Margaret (Anon.), 178-180.
Marget [= Margaret], 213.
Marius (A. Ramsay), 185.
Martialis, M. V., 4.
Lady Mary, 135, Lady M. W. Montagu.
Miss Mary (M. Prior), 76, 77.
Mary, the Cook - Maid [= Scullery Maid] (Dean J. Swift), 212, 213.
Matthew, 91, Matthew Prior.
May, 202, Maid.
Meander's banks, 86.
Mechlin pendants, 189, cuffs of Mechlin lace.
Megrim [= headache] (A. Pope), 24.

Meikle, 181, great.
Whirling Mill, 15, 20, the coffee-mill.
Miller, Rev. J., 265.
Milton, J., 21, 299.
The Mincio [= a tributary of the Po], 39.
Mint, 132, a district in London formerly largely inhabited by poor scribblers.
Mint, 182, meant.
Mira (Anon.), 258-260.
Miranda (A. Finch, Countess of Winchilsea), 111.
Mistress, always, in this Series, in a good sense; with its many equivalents, such as, sweet Heart! &c.
Mizella (A. Phipps), 106.
Molly (M. Prior), 85.
Molly Mog (J. Gay), 167-169.
Momentilla, a Sylph (A. Pope), 14.
Monk, Hon. M., 137.
Montagu, Lord Halifax; C., 38, 44.
Montagu, Lady M. W., 135, 143-146, 150-155.
Montfaucon, the French Antiquary; B. de, 132.
Mordaunt, Earl of Peterborough; C., 225.
Mordaunt (W. Popple), 251.
Morley, Mrs. [= Thalestris], 26, 27, 30-32.
Motteux, P. A., 66, 67.
Myra (Rev. L. Eusden, P.L.), 136.
Myra [= F. Livingstone, Countess of Newburgh] (G. Granville, Lord Lansdowne), 239, 241.
Myra (G. Lyttelton, Lord Lansdowne), 246.
Myrtle (H. Baker, F.R.S.), 231.

Na, 183, 185, 202, &c., no, not.
Nae mair, 185, no more.
Nancy (Archdeacon T. Parnell, D.D.), 114, 115.
Nancy, Nanny (C. Hamilton, Lord Binning), 242, 243.
Nappy, 222, strong, heady ale.
The Nar [= Nera], 39.
Nassau [= King William III] (Rt. Hon. J. Addison), 40, 44.
Nathing, 202, nothing.
Ne, 202, not.
Ne'er, 60, 67, 155, &c., never.
The Nile, 40.
Nisus, 20.
The doctrine of Non Resistance to Kings, when oppressors, 148.
The North, 90, Denmark, Sweden, &c.
Nothing, 265.
Numbers, 39, 81, 108, &c., Poetry.
Nymphs, see Machines, 6.

Ods-fish! 92, God's fish!
O'er, 3, 12, &c., over.
Ombre, 6, 17-19, 129, 189, a game of cards.
Laid on board, 99, defeated in duelling.
Oped, 5, opened.
Orpheus, 110, 214.
Othello (W. Shakespeare), 34.
My outer fabric, 185, my body.
Ovidius Naso, P., 4, 20.

Paget, Lord Paget; T. C., 292, 293.
Pain (A. Pope), 24.
Panthea (Anon.), 97, 98.
Paris, 71.
Parnell, D.D.; Archdeacon T., 114-120.
Parsonable [= personable], 212, a man of good presence.
Parthenissa (Capt. Sir R. Steele), 62, 63.
Partridge, J., 35, the London Astrologer who had been recently so mercilessly ridiculed by Swift under the name of Isaac Bickerstaff.
Passion, predilection, habitude. 'The ruling Passion strong in death.'
Passion, emotion, not necessarily of love. It might also be of anger, grief, zeal, &c.
Passion, Passions, anxieties of mind and agonies of soul through love for one of the opposite sex.
Passive Obedience, 148, to the King as the Lord's Anointed.
Pastora (J. Thurston), 226.
So pat, 171, to the point.
Sees them patch, 99, put Patches on their faces.
Patch-box, 29, box of Patches.
Patches, 9, small round spots of black silk put by Ladies on their faces.
Queen, and a lasting Peace, 37. This fixes the date of the writing of this Song. It was written before the Peace of Utrecht, March 30, 1713, O.S.

Glossary and Index.

Penal Law, 147, against Roman Catholics.
Peneus [= Salympria], 157, 158.
Petre, Lord Petre; — (a little man, 5), 4, 11, 18, 19, 20-22, 28, 30, 33, 34.
Phebe (J. Byrom, F.R.S.), 100-103.
Philips, A., 104-108, 134.
Philips, J., 93.
Phillis (E. Howard, Earl of Suffolk), 200.
Phillis (P. Virgilius Maro), 169.
Phillis (W. Walsh), 52, 54
Phyllis (J. Thurston), 226.
On pillions, 176, riding behind a man on horseback.
Pindar, 91.
Plato, 46-48.
Sir Plume [= Sir G. Brown] (A. Pope), 27, 28, 32.
POEMS, ETC.—
Alma, by M. Prior, 91.
The Beggar's Opera, by J. Gay, The Songs in, 170, 171.
Cato, a Tragedy, by the Rt. Hon. J. Addison, 46-49.
The Dunciad, written by A. Pope, 211, 212.
Harmonica Anglica, 1742, and Thesaurus Musicus, 1745, in which the National Anthem first appeared, 274, 275.
The Jovial Crew, written by R. BROME, and altered by E. ROOME; Songs from, 218-220.
Le Lutrin, by N. Boileau-Despreaux, 4.
Nut Brown Maid, by M. Prior, 91.
Rape of the Lock, by A. Pope, 1-35, 109-111.
Rosamond, by Rt. Hon. J. Addison, 45.
Solomon, by M. Prior, 91.
Taste, an Epistle, by A. Pope, 153.
Polly (J. Gay), 171.
Polly (R. Savage), 206.
Polyphemus, 159.
Polytimus (M. V. Martialis), 4.
Poortith, 181, poverty.
Pope, A., 1-36, 46-47, 109, 132, 135, 150, 151, 210-212.
Popple, W., 251.
Poppling stream, 185, bubbling.
Pother, 202, bustle.
Pottle Pot, 130, a pot containing half a gallon.

Powder, 14, for the face, or hair.
A Prelate for wit, &c., 134, Bishop F. Atterbury.
Wi' poortith prest, 184, oppressed with poverty.
Young Pretender, 275, Prince C. E. Stuart.
Inferior Priestess, 9, Betty, the lady's-maid.
Prior, M., 68-92, 132, 135.
Procullus, 35.
Prudentia (C. Mordaunt, Earl of Peterborough), 225.
In pudding time, 148, in the nick of time, the critical moment.
Purling, 224, rippling.
Puss, 216, a popular name for the hare.
Pygmalion, 238.

Quadrille, 224, 271, a game of cards.
The Queen, 37, Queen Anne.
Quite a', 185, quit all.

R. S., 194, 195.
Ramsay, A., 181-185.
Raphael, 42, S. Raffaelle.
Young Rattles, 177, loud, foolish talkers.
The Red [Coat], 65, the Officers of the Army.
Redlynch Park, Somerset, 288.
The Revolution of 1688, 147.
Riggs, 181, hills.
The Ring, 6, 27, 190, 270, a circular carriage drive in Hyde Park, London.
Rivelled, 15, shrivelled.
Robin [= the poetical name of C. Hamilton, Lord Binning], 242, 243.
Rome, 41.
Roome, E., 218-220.
Rosamond's Lake in St. James' Park, London, 35.
'Rose, 220, arose.
Rowe, P. L.; N., 124-127.
Russet [= a reddish-brown colour], 223, a home-spun gown.

'S, 3, 37, &c., is.
'S, 37, 66, 228, &c., us.
Sabina (W. Congreve), 57.
Sabina (Archdeacon T. Parnell, D.D.), 119.
Sackville, Earl of Dorset; C., 92.
Saint Osyth, 291, in Essex.
Salamanders, see Machines, 6.

Salisbury, 112.
Sally [= Sarah] (H. Carey), 266-268.
Sally (Rev. J. Hoadly), 254, 255.
Sappho, Songs by, 104-106.
Sappho (C. Mordaunt, Earl of Peterborough), 225.
Sapphos, 109, Poetesses.
Saul, 185, soul.
Savage, R., 206, 207.
Scylla, 20.
Semele (W. Congreve), 58.
Seraphina (J. Thomson), 284.
Shakespeare, W., 299.
She, the emphatic feminine Personal Pronoun, used where the poetical name of the Lady does not occur.
She'd, 60, 97, 200, &c., she would.
Sheffield, Duke of Buckingham; J., 131-135.
She'll, 76, 77, 182, &c., she will.
Sheridan, D.D.; Rev. T., 212, 213.
Sherlock, R., 212.
Shippen, M.P.; —, 134, the incorruptible Jacobite.
Sic, 183, 202, such.
Side-Box, 30, of a theatre, filled with Gentlemen bowing to the Ladies in the Front Box.
Silver token, 5 — see V, 150.
Silvia (A. Finch, Countess of Winchilsea), 111.
Silvio (Anon.), 233-235.
Simmer, 182, summer.
Sirrah! 72, an angry, or contemptuous, exclamation.
Skair, 185, share.
Sma' folk [= small people], 184, the middle class.
A snush-box, 71, snuff-box.
Soe'er, 52, soever.
Somervile, W., 214-217.
The Sound must seem an echo to the Sense, 3.
Southerne, T., 135.
South Sea, 175-177, the Pacific Ocean.
South Sea Babel, or Bubble, 177, 188, the speculations for fisheries, &c., &c., in the Pacific Ocean, of 1720.
Spain, 90, 262, 263.
Sparks, 7, 181, Gallants.
Speer na, 185, enquire not.
Spleen, a Goddess (A. Pope), 23-26.
Spleen, 144, dejection, melancholy.
Springes, 11, shares.
Vulgar springs, 46, motives.
'Spying, 135, espying.

311

Glossary and Index.

Squairly, 185, squarely.
The Stagyrite, 90, Aristotle.
H: st iw, 195, he stole.
Fragrant steams, 21, of the coffee.
Steele, Capt. Sir R., 62, 63, 133.
Stella [=? Esther Johnson] (M. Barber), 221.
Stella (M. Prior), 88.
Stowe, 248, 249, co. Bucks.
Straight, 65, immediately, at once
Strait [= straight], 20, immediately.
Straths, 184, valleys.
Strephon (Anon.), 233-235.
Strephon (Anon.), 258-260.
Strephon (W. Bedingfield), 156, 157.
Strephon (R. Leveridge), 264.
Strephon (Lady M. W. Montagu), 145.
Strephon (A. Philips), 108.
Strephon (E. Roome), 218.
Stuart, Mrs. (H. Carey), 276.
Surly (Anon.), 98, 99.
Black-eyed Susan (J. Gay), 160 162.
The Swede, 44, Sweden.
Swift, Dean J., 135, 210-213.
Swig, 268, drink.
Take my swing, 224, enjoy myself thoroughly.
Sword-knots, 8, 12, knotted ribbands or tassels tied to sword-hilts.
Sylphs, Sylphids, see Machines, 5, 12-15, 17, 20, 12, 32, 35.
Sylvia (A. Pope), 12.
Sylvia (W. Walsh), 52.

In a pitiful taking, 143, in a great perplexity, quandary.
Tauk, 183, talk.
The Tay, 184, the largest river in Scotland.
Temple, Sir W., 125.
Th', 3, 11, 12, &c., the.
Thalestris [= Mrs. Morley] (A. Pope), 4, 26, 27, 30-32.
Silver Thames, 10, 16, 86, &c.
They'll, 149, they will.
They're, 149, they are.
They'se, 181, they will.
They've, 149, they have.
Tho', 194, though.
Thomas (Rev. J. Hoadly), 254, 255.
Thomson, J., 278-284.
Thou'rt, 154, thou art.
Thurston, J., 226, 227.
Thyrsis (G. Granville, Lord Lansdowne), 240, 241.

Thyrsis (Archdeacon T. Parnell, D.D.), 119.
Gentle Tiber, 40.
Tickell, T., 172-174.
'Tis, 3, 7, 45, &c., it is.
A Toast, 30, 84, 124, &c., a Beauty, a Belle.
Modern Toasting, 67, drinking the Healths of Beauties and Queens of Society.
Well-tochered Lasses, 181, dowered.
Tonson, the Publisher; J., 124, 125, 132.
T' other, 165, 170, 177, &c., the other.
Toupees, 204, 258, 270, small wigs, artificial curls or locks.
Town, 108 (London Town, 110), 133, 192, &c., the London fashionable World.
Toyshop, 8, a haberdashery shop for Ladies (not a place for children's toys).
Train, 12, company.
Train, 17, 215, 220, &c., attendants.
Tr—p, 134.
Troy, 22, 72.
Tully—see Cicero, M. T.
'Twas, 5, 55, 100, &c., it was.
The river Tweed, 184.
'Twill, 155, it will.
Twitched, 92, plucked.

Ulysses, 26.
Umbria, 40.
Umbriel, a Gnome, see Machines, 23-26, 28, 32.
Treaty of Utrecht, 37, 91.

Vanbrugh, Capt. Sir J., 124, 125, 134.
Professor Van der Bruin, 75.
Vapours, 25, 144, dejection, melancholy.
Velvet plain, 17, verdant Field, 18, level Green, 19. It would seem that the cardtable was covered with green velvet.
Venus, 35, the Planet.
Vials [= phials], 15, 26, 28, medicine bottles.
Virenia (E. Howard, Earl of Suffolk), 201.
Virgilius Maro, P., 38, 40, 44, 169.
Vittels, 213, victuals.

Wad, 202, would.
Wade, Marshal, 275.
Wadna, 183, would not
Wadst, 183, wouldst.
Wair'd, 183, spent.

The wale, 184, the best.
Waller, E., 3.
Walsh, W., 52-54.
Waltham Cross, 219.
Ward, E., 175-177.
Wash, 14, a hair Wash.
Waterland, D.D.; Rev. D., 90.
We'll, 37, 59, &c., we will.
Welsted, L., 138, 139.
We're, 155, we are.
Wesley the Elder, Rev. S., 199.
West, R., 285-287.
Westminster Abbey, 209.
Whaever, 184, whoever.
Where'er, 3, wherever.
White minute, 183, favourable opportunity, as happy minute, 196.
White Rods [= White Staffs] in Waiting, 64.
White's Chocolate House, now White's Club, St. James' Street, London, 64, 108.
Who've, 177, who have.
Will-a-wisp, 167, Ignis fatuus, marsh gas.
William (Anon.), 178-180.
Sweet William (J. Gay), 160-162.
King William III, 40, 44, 91, 148.
Williams, K.B.; Sir C. H., 288-291.
Will's [= William Urwin's Coffee House, in Russell Street, Covent Garden, London], 108.
Willy, 203, wily.
They wimple, 184, meander.
Winifreda (Anon.), 208, 209.
Ere he wist, 183, before he knew.
Withoutten, 184, without.

Yarrow, 196, 197, Yarrow Water in Selkirkshire.
Y—g, 134, ? Rt. Hon. Sir W. Yonge, Bart.
Yonge, Bart.; Rt. Hon. Sir W., 236, 237.
You'd, 60, 206, &c., you would.
You'll, 11, you will.
You're, 98, 143, 206, &c., you are.
You've, 137, 143, 228, &c., you have.

Zelinda (A. Philips), 106.
Zelinda (L. Welsted), 138, 139.
Zephyretta, a Sylph (A. Pope), 14.

www.ingramcontent.com/pod-product-compliance
Lightning Source LLC
Chambersburg PA
CBHW030811230426
43667CB00008B/1169